Photoshop Lightroom Classic 2025 User Guide

Unlock Pro-Level Editing with Expert Techniques

SOPHIE KELBY

Photoshop Lightroom Classic 2025 User Guide

Unlock Pro-Level Editing with Expert Techniques

SOPHIE KELBY

DISCLAIMER

The information provided in *Photoshop Lightroom Classic 2025 User Guide: Unlock Pro-Level Editing with Expert Techniques* is intended for educational and informational purposes only. While every effort has been made to ensure the accuracy of the content, the author and publisher make no warranties or representations regarding the completeness or accuracy of the material.

The techniques and advice presented in this book are based on the author's experience with Photoshop Lightroom Classic 2025 as of the publication date. Due to continuous updates and changes to the software, the author and publisher do not assume any responsibility for any differences in future versions of the software.

The use of the information contained within this book is at the reader's own risk. The author and publisher will not be liable for any damages, losses, or injuries resulting from the use of this information, including but not limited to technical issues, software errors, or mistakes in the application of the techniques.

The reader is encouraged to back up their data and ensure that their systems are properly configured and protected before implementing any of the techniques or suggestions outlined in this book.

Adobe, Lightroom, and other related product names are trademarks or registered trademarks of Adobe Inc. This book is not affiliated with, endorsed by, or sponsored by Adobe Inc. or any other third-party organizations mentioned within.

HOW TO USE THIS GUIDE

Welcome to the *Photoshop Lightroom Classic 2025 User Guide: Unlock Pro-Level Editing with Expert Techniques*! Whether you're a beginner or an advanced photographer, this guide is crafted to help you master Lightroom Classic 2025 and enhance your photo editing skills. Here's how you can effectively use this guide to get the most out of it:

1. Guide Structure:

- **Chapters & Subchapters:** The book is organized into chapters, each covering a distinct aspect of Lightroom Classic 2025. Chapters start with fundamental concepts and progress to more advanced topics. You can read the chapters sequentially to build your skills or use them as standalone references if you need to focus on specific areas.

- **Flow:** Each chapter follows a structured approach, starting with an introduction and key concepts, followed by detailed instructions and tips. End-of-chapter summaries and key takeaways help reinforce the learning.

2. Navigating the Table of Contents:

- The **Table of Contents** provides a comprehensive list of chapters and subchapters. Use this to quickly locate the topic you're interested in, whether it's basic setup, advanced editing techniques, or troubleshooting issues.

3. Using Visual Aids:

- **Screenshots and Diagrams** are used throughout the guide to illustrate key concepts. Follow these visuals closely to see exactly where to click and what settings to adjust in Lightroom.

- **Diagrams** break down complex workflows and are essential for understanding new tools and techniques.

4. Practical Application:

- Each chapter includes **real-world tips and exercises** to apply what you've learned. These exercises are designed to reinforce skills through practice and experimentation with Lightroom's features.

- **Case studies** and tips in various chapters will help you understand how to integrate Lightroom tools into your regular workflow.

5. Quick Reference for Advanced Topics:

- **Advanced Techniques** such as color grading, retouching, and image restoration are covered in later chapters. You can refer to these chapters once you've mastered the basics, or dive directly into them if you want to elevate your editing skills immediately.

6. Customizing Your Workflow:

- This guide offers recommendations for **customizing Lightroom** to fit your workflow. From setting up the interface and preferences to using presets and managing catalogs, you'll learn how to tailor Lightroom to your editing needs.

7. Tips for Efficient Reading:

- **Skip to What Interests You:** Feel free to jump ahead if you're already familiar with certain concepts and want to focus on more advanced techniques.

- **Revisit Chapters:** Revisit chapters or subchapters for deeper exploration, especially as you become more comfortable with the software and its tools.

8. Final Recommendations:

- **Practice Makes Perfect:** To truly unlock Lightroom's potential, continue to practice with your own photos. Experiment with different tools, settings, and techniques to become more confident in your editing skills.

TABLE OF CONTENTS

INTRODUCTION 10

    Welcome to Lightroom Classic 2025 USER GUIDE 10

    What's New in Lightroom Classic 2025? 11

CHAPTER 1: GETTING STARTED WITH LIGHTROOM CLASSIC 2025 14

    Introduction to Lightroom Classic 14

    Setting Up Your Workspace 15

    Importing Your First Photos 16

    Understanding the Catalog and Library Modules 17

    Organizing Your Photos with Folders and Collections 19

CHAPTER 2: THE LIBRARY MODULE – ORGANIZING AND MANAGING PHOTOS 22

    Importing and Exporting Images 22

    Rating, Flagging, and Labeling Your Images 24

    Using Metadata and Keywords for Easy Search 25

    Advanced Photo Organization Techniques 27

    Smart Collections and Filters 28

CHAPTER 3: THE DEVELOP MODULE – EDITING BASICS 30

    Introduction to the Develop Module 30

    Basic Editing Tools: Exposure, Contrast, and Clarity 31

    Understanding the Tone Curve for Better Control 32

    Color Adjustments: White Balance and HSL Panel 34

    Applying and Using Presets for Faster Workflow 35

    Cropping and Straightening Your Images 36

CHAPTER 4: MASTERING ADVANCED EDITING TECHNIQUES 38

    Using the Graduated Filter and Radial Filter for Selective Edits 38

Introduction to the Adjustment Brush for Fine-Tuning 39

Working with the Range Mask for More Control 40

Advanced Color Grading Techniques 42

Using the Tone Curve for Precision Control 43

How to Achieve Stunning Black and White Conversions 43

CHAPTER 5: ADVANCED RETOUCHING AND IMAGE RESTORATION 46

Spot Removal and Healing Tools for Flawless Images 46

Using the Clone Tool for Precision Editing 48

Reducing Noise and Sharpening Your Images 50

Working with the Dehaze Tool 51

Skin Retouching and Portrait Editing Techniques 52

CHAPTER 6: MASTERING MASKING IN LIGHTROOM CLASSIC 54

Introduction to Masking Techniques 54

Creating and Refining Masks in Lightroom 55

Using the New Masking Tools in Lightroom Classic 2025 56

Color and Luminance Masking for Precision Control 57

Brush Masking vs. Gradient Masking: When to Use Each 58

CHAPTER 7: ADVANCED WORKFLOW AND EFFICIENCY TIPS 60

Setting Up Your Lightroom Preferences for Maximum Speed 60

Efficient File Management and Backup Strategies 61

Using Virtual Copies to Experiment Without Losing Original Shots 63

Synchronizing Settings Across Multiple Images 64

Batch Editing: How to Save Time with Presets and Syncing 65

CHAPTER 8: INTEGRATING LIGHTROOM WITH OTHER ADOBE TOOLS 68

Using Lightroom with Photoshop for Advanced Editing 68

Exporting and Preparing Images for Print or Web 69

Syncing Lightroom with Adobe Creative Cloud 71

Smart Previews: Working Without Original Files 72

Lightroom Mobile Integration and Editing on the Go...........................73

CHAPTER 9: TROUBLESHOOTING AND COMMON LIGHTROOM ISSUES
....76

Solving Performance Issues and Speed Optimization 76

Resolving Import and Export Problems...78

How to Fix Corrupted Catalogs 80

Common Editing Mistakes and How to Fix Them 81

Backup and Restore: Protecting Your Catalog and Edits 82

CHAPTER 10: PRO TIPS FOR CREATING STUNNING FINAL IMAGES.......84

Color Grading for Cinematic Looks 84

Creative Effects: Vignettes, Split Toning, and More 86

Enhancing Details with the Clarity and Texture Sliders.......................88

Finalizing Your Workflow for Consistency 89

Exporting for Professional Results 90

APPENDICES 92

Glossary of Lightroom Classic Terms 92

Keyboard Shortcuts for Faster Editing 94

Recommended Resources and Further Reading....................................95

Troubleshooting Guide for Lightroom Classic 2025.............................98

INTRODUCTION

WELCOME TO LIGHTROOM CLASSIC 2025 USER GUIDE

Photography has always been more than just taking pictures. It's about capturing a moment, telling a story, and creating something that resonates with the viewer. But as photographers, whether you're a hobbyist or a professional, your work doesn't end when you press the shutter button. The true magic often happens after the shot—when you enhance, refine, and perfect your images. That's where Adobe Lightroom Classic comes in.

For years, Lightroom Classic has been the go-to tool for photographers of all levels, offering an array of powerful editing features that allow you to transform your raw images into works of art. With the release of Lightroom Classic 2025, Adobe has continued to push the boundaries of what's possible in digital photo editing, introducing new features, updates, and improvements that make it an even more invaluable tool in your photography workflow. Whether you're a seasoned pro or a beginner looking to take your photography skills to the next level, this guide will help you navigate Lightroom Classic 2025 and master its features.

The journey of photo editing can be overwhelming at first—there are so many tools, sliders, and options, each offering endless possibilities. But with Lightroom Classic 2025, you'll quickly find that each feature is designed with a purpose: to help you create the perfect image. This guide is here to walk you through the process, step by step, giving you the confidence to take control of your editing process and unlock the full potential of your images. From organizing your photos to advanced editing techniques, you'll learn everything you need to know to become a Lightroom expert.

Photography is not just about having the best equipment; it's about understanding how to use the tools available to you effectively. And Lightroom Classic 2025 is one of the best tools a photographer can have at their disposal. With its powerful suite of features and user-friendly interface, it allows you to do everything from basic adjustments to complex image manipulation, all while preserving the quality of your photographs. But, like any great tool, it takes time and practice to fully harness its potential. This guide is the perfect starting point for that journey.

In this book, you'll find expert techniques that will not only enhance your images but also streamline your editing workflow. You'll learn to use Lightroom Classic like a pro, mastering advanced editing methods, automating your processes, and improving your efficiency. By the end, you'll be able to make the most of every image, no matter your photography style or editing goals. Let's dive into the world of Lightroom Classic 2025 and unlock pro-level editing with expert techniques.

WHAT'S NEW IN LIGHTROOM CLASSIC 2025?

With each new version of Lightroom Classic, Adobe continues to refine the software and add new features that enhance its already powerful capabilities. Lightroom Classic 2025 is no exception, and in this chapter, we'll highlight some of the key updates and improvements that make this release stand out. If you've been using Lightroom Classic for a while, you'll notice some exciting changes that will improve your workflow and creative options.

One of the most significant updates to Lightroom Classic 2025 is the **new masking tools**. Adobe has introduced a revamped version of its masking system, which now includes even more precision and control over local adjustments. With these new tools, you can create highly detailed masks for specific areas of your image, allowing you to target precise parts of the photo for adjustments like exposure, contrast, and color grading. Whether you're working with landscapes, portraits, or product photography, these improvements will give you the flexibility to make more complex edits that were previously difficult or time-consuming.

Another exciting feature is **enhanced AI-powered editing**. Adobe has implemented several AI-driven tools in Lightroom Classic 2025, such as automatic color grading, noise reduction, and enhanced sharpening. These features use machine learning to analyze your photos and make intelligent adjustments that improve the overall quality of your images. Whether you're editing portraits or landscapes, the AI tools in Lightroom Classic 2025 will help you get stunning results faster and with less manual input.

Lightroom Classic 2025 has also improved its **exporting and file management** capabilities. Now, you can export images in batches with more flexibility, including new presets that make it easier to save time when exporting multiple images for web, print, or social media. The updated **organizational tools** help streamline your workflow by allowing for more efficient sorting, tagging, and searching of images. Plus, Lightroom now offers more **cloud integration**, so you can seamlessly sync your photos across devices and platforms, making it easier to edit on the go.

Additionally, Lightroom Classic 2025 has introduced a more **intuitive user interface**, with clearer menu options, streamlined controls, and new customization features. These updates make it easier to navigate the software and tailor the interface to your specific needs. With these changes, Lightroom Classic 2025 feels faster, more responsive, and more accessible to photographers of all skill levels.

Finally, Adobe has also made improvements to the **performance and stability** of Lightroom Classic. The software now runs more smoothly, especially when handling large catalogs or high-resolution images. These optimizations mean that Lightroom Classic 2025 will run faster, reducing lag and allowing you to spend more time editing and less time waiting for the program to catch up.

All in all, Lightroom Classic 2025 represents a significant leap forward in photo editing software. Whether you're just starting out or you've been using Lightroom for years, the new features and updates will help you elevate your editing game. In this guide, we'll explore each of these new features in detail, showing you how to incorporate them into your editing workflow and get the most out of Lightroom Classic 2025.

As you embark on your journey through this guide, remember that mastering Lightroom Classic 2025 is a gradual process. Take your time, experiment with the tools, and most importantly, have fun with it. Photography is about expressing yourself and telling a story, and Lightroom Classic gives you the freedom to bring your vision to life in ways you might not have thought possible.

In the chapters to come, we'll dive into everything from basic photo organization and management to advanced editing techniques that will elevate your work. We'll walk you through each feature step by step, providing expert tips, tricks, and shortcuts that will help you become a more efficient and effective Lightroom user.

By the time you finish this guide, you'll be able to edit photos with confidence, speed, and precision, and you'll be able to unlock the true power of Lightroom Classic 2025. Let's begin your journey into the world of pro-level photo editing!

CHAPTER 1: GETTING STARTED WITH LIGHTROOM CLASSIC 2025

INTRODUCTION TO LIGHTROOM CLASSIC

In the world of photography, post-production is just as important as the shoot itself. Whether you're a beginner looking to refine your skills or a professional aiming to take your photos to the next level, the tools you use to edit and organize your photos can make all the difference. Adobe Lightroom Classic has been one of the most trusted and versatile editing and organizing tools available for photographers worldwide. With its latest update, Lightroom Classic 2025 takes the software's capabilities even further, offering photographers a more powerful, efficient, and creative editing experience.

Lightroom Classic is renowned for its combination of non-destructive editing, a vast range of powerful tools, and robust photo management features. Unlike other photo editing software, Lightroom allows you to make adjustments to your images without permanently altering the original files. This non-destructive workflow is one of the core reasons Lightroom has become a staple in the professional photography community. Whether you're working with RAW, TIFF, or JPEG files, you can rest assured that your original image will remain intact while you experiment with adjustments, filters, and edits.

What sets Lightroom Classic apart from other editing programs is its seamless integration of two essential functions: organizing and editing photos. The Library and Develop modules work hand-in-hand to help photographers store, sort, and process their images in an intuitive, user-friendly interface. Lightroom Classic empowers photographers to streamline their workflows, improve efficiency, and focus more on creativity.

For those new to Lightroom, it might seem overwhelming at first with its array of panels, sliders, and options. But once you understand the core concepts of Lightroom, you'll quickly realize how it can simplify and enhance your post-processing. In this chapter, we will explore the foundational aspects of Lightroom Classic 2025, so you can set up your workspace, import and organize your photos, and get comfortable with the essential features that will lay the groundwork for your editing journey.

SETTING UP YOUR WORKSPACE

When you first launch Lightroom Classic 2025, you're presented with a clean, organized interface that may seem intimidating. But don't worry—this section will help you get comfortable with the layout and tools available. Properly setting up your workspace is key to working efficiently in Lightroom. With the right setup, you can maximize your workflow and ensure that your editing process is as smooth as possible.

The Interface Breakdown

The Lightroom Classic workspace is divided into several key panels, each serving a unique function. At the top of the screen, you'll find the **Module Picker**—this is where you can switch between Lightroom's main modules, including Library, Develop, Map, Slideshow, Print, and Web. The **Library** and **Develop** modules are where you will spend most of your time, so understanding these two areas is crucial.

Below the Module Picker, you'll see the **Toolbar**. This is where you can access tools like the Crop tool, Red Eye tool, and Spot Removal tool, which are commonly used for editing images. On the left-hand side, you'll find the **Panels** which provide access to photo collections, folders, keywords, and metadata. The right-hand side hosts the **Develop Panel**, where you can fine-tune adjustments, apply presets, and enhance your images.

Customizing Your Workspace

One of Lightroom's most powerful features is its customizability. The default workspace is designed to be clean and functional, but you can personalize it to suit your editing style and preferences. You can adjust the size of the panels, move them around, and even create custom workspaces for different tasks. For instance, you might want a larger preview area in the Develop module when you're focusing on detailed retouching or a more compact Library module for organizing large sets of photos.

Another workspace customization option is the ability to show or hide panels. If you prefer a minimalist interface, you can collapse panels you don't need at the moment.

This flexibility makes Lightroom Classic adaptable to your needs, allowing you to focus only on the tools that are essential for your current task.

Setting Up Preferences

Before diving into photo editing, it's a good idea to adjust Lightroom's preferences to match your workflow. To access preferences, simply go to the **Edit** menu on Windows or **Lightroom** on Mac, then choose **Preferences**. Here, you can customize a range of settings that will affect how Lightroom Classic operates.

You can set default behavior for importing images, choose which color space to use for editing, adjust the performance settings for speed optimization, and configure backup settings to ensure your catalog is always safe. Tailoring these preferences to your needs will help Lightroom run more smoothly and speed up your workflow.

Once your workspace is set up, it's time to start working with images. Lightroom Classic 2025 is all about efficient management and editing, and this next section will guide you through importing your first batch of photos.

IMPORTING YOUR FIRST PHOTOS

The first step in working with Lightroom Classic is importing your photos into the software. Lightroom uses a non-destructive editing workflow, which means that your original images are never altered during the editing process. Instead, Lightroom stores your edits as metadata in its catalog, allowing you to make changes without damaging the source file.

Navigating the Import Dialog

To begin importing photos, click the **Import** button in the Library module. This opens the **Import Dialog Box**, where you can select the source of your photos. Lightroom allows you to import images from several sources, including memory cards, external hard drives, or even directly from a camera.

Once you've chosen your source, you'll see thumbnails of the images you're about to import. This is a great time to select only the images you want to work with, avoiding clutter in your catalog later on. Lightroom offers several import options, such as applying metadata, adding keywords, or even selecting a destination folder where your images will be stored.

Choosing Import Settings

Lightroom Classic offers several settings you can adjust during the import process:

1. **File Handling**: Choose whether you want Lightroom to copy, move, or add your images to the catalog. Copying is the safest option, as it creates a backup of your files in your chosen destination folder. If you're confident in your file management system, you can opt to move the images.

2. **File Renaming**: Lightroom gives you the option to rename your files upon import. This can be useful if you want to organize your images by project name, date, or custom naming conventions.

3. **Apply During Import**: You can apply adjustments or presets right as the photos are imported. For instance, you can add a sharpening preset or apply basic exposure corrections to all images.

4. **Destination Folder**: Organizing your photos during import is crucial. Lightroom gives you the ability to specify a destination folder for the imported images, which is a good opportunity to start organizing your files right from the start.

Tips for a Smooth Import Process

To make the importing process efficient, always make sure that your images are well-organized before importing them into Lightroom. Keep folders named logically and create a folder structure that works for your workflow. Additionally, Lightroom allows you to apply metadata and keywords during the import process, which can help you quickly find images later on. This is especially useful if you work with large numbers of images from different shoots.

After you've imported your images, Lightroom will automatically generate a preview, and you'll be able to start working with them right away. The next step is organizing your images effectively.

UNDERSTANDING THE CATALOG AND LIBRARY MODULES

Once your images are imported, they are stored in a **catalog**. A catalog is a database where Lightroom keeps track of your images and all the changes you make to them. Unlike traditional photo editing software that works directly on the images themselves, Lightroom Classic maintains a catalog of images and stores metadata (like edits, ratings, and keywords) separately. This means you can always revert to the original photo without losing any information.

The Catalog

Think of the catalog as the central hub of Lightroom. It doesn't store the actual image files (unless you specifically export them), but instead contains all the necessary data about those files. The catalog stores information about each photo's location on your computer, its metadata, and the edits you've applied. Every time you open Lightroom, you load your catalog, which allows you to access all your images and the edits you've made to them.

You can have multiple catalogs, each dedicated to different projects or workflows, but it's generally recommended to keep a single catalog for better organization. Lightroom makes it easy to import, export, and back up your catalog, ensuring that your work is safe and accessible.

The Library Module

The Library module is where you manage and organize your photos. It's where you'll spend a lot of time sorting through your images, applying keywords, and categorizing them for easy retrieval. In this module, you'll find several key tools for organizing your photos:

- **Grid View**: The grid view allows you to see thumbnails of all your images in a folder or collection, making it easy to navigate through large numbers of photos.

- **Loupe View**: This gives you a closer look at an individual image. You can zoom in on your photo to inspect details and make editing decisions.

- **Filter Bar**: The filter bar lets you quickly sort through your images based on attributes such as flags, ratings, and keywords.

- **Collections and Folders**: You can organize your images into collections, which are virtual folders that help you group photos for specific projects, themes, or edits. Collections are a great way to stay organized and easily find photos when you need them.

ORGANIZING YOUR PHOTOS WITH FOLDERS AND COLLECTIONS

As your catalog grows, it becomes increasingly important to have a system in place for organizing your images. Lightroom Classic 2025 offers two primary methods for organizing photos: **folders** and **collections**. Let's take a look at both.

Folders

Folders are where your images physically reside on your hard drive. When you import your photos into Lightroom, they are placed into a folder that exists on your computer's file system. Lightroom tracks the location of these folders, making it easy to organize your files and access them from within the program. You can create subfolders for each shoot or project and move images around as needed.

Collections

Collections are a virtual organization system within Lightroom Classic. Unlike folders, collections don't physically move or alter your images—they simply allow you to group them together in a way that makes sense for your workflow. For example, you might create a collection for your best photos from a shoot, a collection for images that need further editing, or a collection for images that are ready for export.

You can also create **Smart Collections**, which automatically group images based on specific criteria. For example, you could create a Smart Collection that contains all images with a 5-star rating, or one that only includes images tagged with a particular keyword.

With both folders and collections, Lightroom Classic 2025 makes it easier than ever to stay organized and efficient. By the time you finish this chapter, you'll be ready to dive into the more advanced editing techniques that Lightroom has to offer, all while knowing how to keep your photos well-organized and easily accessible.

Getting started with Lightroom Classic 2025 may seem like a big task, but once you've set up your workspace, imported and organized your photos, and understood the catalog system, you'll find that the software becomes an invaluable tool in your workflow. By mastering the basics of the Library module, understanding how to manage your images, and organizing your photos with folders and collections, you'll be well on your way to becoming a Lightroom pro.

In the next chapters, we'll delve deeper into the **Develop module**, where the real magic of photo editing happens. But for now, you're ready to start experimenting with Lightroom's powerful organizational tools and prepare your images for the creative journey ahead.

CHAPTER 2: THE LIBRARY MODULE – ORGANIZING AND MANAGING PHOTOS

IMPORTING AND EXPORTING IMAGES

When it comes to organizing and managing your photos in Lightroom Classic 2025, one of the first essential steps is getting your images into the program. Whether you're working from a camera, an external hard drive, or cloud storage, knowing how to import and export images efficiently will lay the foundation for a smooth editing and workflow process. Lightroom is known for its ability to handle large volumes of photos with ease, making it a powerful tool for photographers who need to manage vast libraries of images.

The Import Process

The import process in Lightroom Classic is straightforward yet powerful, offering various options to suit your needs. When you first launch Lightroom, you'll find yourself in the **Library** module, where all the organizing and managing magic happens. To import photos, simply click the **Import** button located in the lower-left corner of the Library module. This will open the **Import Dialog Box**, where you can select the source of your images. You can import images from several sources, including memory cards, external hard drives, and even cloud storage services if they're linked to Lightroom.

The first thing you'll notice is the **Source** panel, which shows the available drives and devices. Lightroom also allows you to import images directly from your camera, and in some cases, even from a connected smartphone. Once you've selected the source, you'll see thumbnails of the images you wish to import. You can then preview each image to ensure that you're only bringing in the best shots. Lightroom allows you to either **Copy** (to create duplicates of your images in a new location), **Move** (to relocate your images to a new location), or **Add** (which simply adds the images to the Lightroom catalog without copying them).

It's important to note that Lightroom's cataloging system is at the heart of its workflow. The program doesn't store images in the catalog itself; it only tracks their location, along with all the metadata and edits you apply. This non-destructive workflow ensures that the original files are never altered, while you can freely edit and experiment with your images within Lightroom.

While importing, you'll also be given several options to further refine your import settings. For example, you can choose to apply **Develop Presets** during the import process. If you have a preset that you use often, such as a basic exposure correction or color grading setup, you can apply it immediately upon import. This can save you valuable time, especially when dealing with large batches of images.

Additionally, you can rename files during import by setting custom file naming rules. Lightroom also gives you the option to add **metadata** and **keywords** upon import, which will help you stay organized right from the start. We'll dive deeper into how to use these tools for effective photo management later in this chapter.

The Export Process

Once your images are organized and edited in Lightroom, the next step is exporting them for sharing, printing, or publishing. The **Export** function is located in the lower-left corner of the Library module, right next to the Import button. The Export dialog offers a wide array of settings to control how your images are saved and shared.

When you select **Export**, Lightroom gives you several options for customization. First, you can specify where the exported files will be saved—whether it's to a specific folder on your computer, an external hard drive, or even directly to a cloud storage service if integrated. You can also set the file format for your export, whether you want to save your images as **JPEG**, **TIFF**, or **PNG** files, among others. This choice depends on your intended use: JPEGs are ideal for web use, while TIFFs offer higher quality for print.

The next step is to define the **Image Settings**. Lightroom allows you to resize your images, adjust their resolution, and control the quality of your exported files. You can also apply **watermarks** to protect your images, as well as set color space preferences for the exported images.

If you're exporting a batch of images, Lightroom also allows you to **add metadata** and apply **output sharpening** to ensure your images look their best when shared or printed. You can even create **export presets** for common output settings, making it easier to export multiple images with the same settings.

Organizing Exports with Folders and Naming Conventions

Just like with importing, the key to an efficient export process lies in organization. Lightroom allows you to define a folder structure for each export, which helps you maintain a clear organizational system for your images after editing. Naming your exported files consistently is also important. Lightroom lets you set up custom naming conventions so that your files are always organized and easy to locate. For example, you could name your images based on the date of the shoot, the client's name, or any other relevant information that will make sense to you.

By understanding both the **import** and **export** processes and using them effectively, you'll be well on your way to mastering Lightroom Classic 2025's organizational features. Importing is the first step in bringing your images into Lightroom, and exporting is the final step in sending them out into the world. Both are crucial to ensuring that your photo management workflow is smooth and efficient.

RATING, FLAGGING, AND LABELING YOUR IMAGES

Organizing your images efficiently in Lightroom Classic requires more than just importing and exporting; it requires thoughtful categorization and easy retrieval. Lightroom offers several methods for **rating**, **flagging**, and **labeling** images, all of which can help you quickly find the best shots and filter out the ones you don't need. Let's dive deeper into these tools and explore how you can leverage them to enhance your workflow.

Rating Your Images

Lightroom Classic provides a simple yet effective **star rating** system to help you assess and rank your images. You can assign up to five stars to each photo based on its quality or relevance. For example, a 5-star rating might signify a top-tier image that you want to use in a portfolio or send to a client, while a 1-star rating could indicate that the image is out of focus or doesn't meet your standards.

To rate an image, simply select it in the **Library** module and press a number on your keyboard (1 to 5). You can also click on the **Rating Stars** in the grid view. This simple system allows you to quickly assign ratings without interrupting your editing process. You can later filter your images based on their ratings, making it easy to locate your best photos or weed out the less-than-perfect ones.

Flagging Your Images

In addition to rating your images, Lightroom also lets you **flag** your photos with either a **Pick** or **Reject** flag. The Pick flag is used to mark images that you want to keep, while the Reject flag indicates images you'd like to discard. This is a great way to quickly identify the best and worst images from a large batch.

You can flag an image by pressing **P** for Pick or **X** for Reject. You can also use the **Flag** icon in the bottom-right corner of the photo. Once you've flagged your images, you can easily filter them by flag status, allowing you to focus on the ones you're interested in and exclude those that didn't make the cut.

Labeling Your Images

Along with ratings and flags, Lightroom also offers **color labels** to further categorize your images. The color labels can be customized to represent different statuses or groups. For example, you might use red for photos that need editing, blue for images you've already retouched, and green for final, approved images. The color labeling system adds another layer of organization, helping you stay on top of your workflow without having to remember which photo is in which stage.

To apply a color label, simply right-click on the image, select **Set Color Label**, and choose the appropriate color. Alternatively, you can use the keyboard shortcuts (6 through 9) to quickly assign color labels.

USING METADATA AND KEYWORDS FOR EASY SEARCH

As your Lightroom catalog grows, it's essential to have an efficient method of finding specific images among thousands of others. This is where **metadata** and **keywords** come into play. Lightroom Classic 2025 offers powerful tools for adding metadata and tagging your images with keywords, allowing you to search and filter your photos with ease. Let's explore how you can use these tools to enhance your photo management process.

Understanding Metadata

Metadata refers to the additional information that Lightroom stores about your images, such as the camera settings used to take the photo, exposure data, and file information. Metadata is automatically applied when you import your images into Lightroom, but you can also manually add or edit metadata to include additional details, such as location, photographer notes, and more.

One of the most useful types of metadata is the **EXIF data** (Exchangeable Image File Format), which contains information about the camera settings used to capture the photo—such as aperture, shutter speed, ISO, and focal length. This data is especially helpful when reviewing your photos to understand how certain settings impacted the shot.

Lightroom allows you to view and edit the metadata for each image in the **Metadata Panel**. You can also choose to display specific metadata fields, depending on what's most relevant to your workflow.

Adding Keywords for Easy Search

Keywords are another crucial component for organizing your photos. They serve as tags that describe the content, location, and context of your images, making it easier to search for them later on. For example, if you shoot landscapes, you might tag your images with keywords like "mountains," "sunset," or "ocean." If you're working on a wedding shoot, you could use keywords like "bride," "groom," or "ceremony."

Adding keywords in Lightroom Classic is easy: simply go to the **Keywording Panel** and type in the relevant keywords for each image. You can also apply multiple keywords to a single image, and Lightroom will automatically suggest related keywords based on the existing tags in your catalog.

Searching with Metadata and Keywords

Once you've tagged your images with metadata and keywords, Lightroom's powerful search capabilities allow you to quickly locate specific photos based on any criteria. In the **Library** module, you can use the **Filter Bar** to search by metadata, flags, ratings, color labels, and keywords. This makes it easy to locate images based on specific attributes—whether you're searching for photos taken with a certain lens, or looking for shots of a particular subject.

You can also create **Saved Filters** for common search criteria, allowing you to save time by quickly retrieving specific sets of images.

ADVANCED PHOTO ORGANIZATION TECHNIQUES

As your Lightroom catalog expands, managing and finding your photos can become more challenging. However, Lightroom Classic 2025 offers several advanced organization techniques that will help you maintain control over your growing library.

Using Collections for Better Organization

In addition to folders, Lightroom Classic also uses **Collections**—virtual groups that allow you to organize your images without changing their physical location. Collections are an excellent way to group photos by project, client, or theme. For example, you can create a collection for a particular wedding shoot, a specific landscape series, or a portfolio for client review.

You can create **Collection Sets** to organize related collections, making it easier to keep everything neatly organized. And best of all, collections don't affect the physical file structure—they simply allow you to group photos together in Lightroom for easier access.

Smart Collections

Smart Collections are even more powerful than regular collections. A **Smart Collection** automatically updates itself based on specific criteria you set. For example, you could create a Smart Collection that includes all images with a 5-star rating, or all photos with the keyword "sunset." The possibilities are endless, and Smart Collections make it easy to automatically organize your images without manual effort.

Using Folders for File Management

While collections are excellent for organizing photos within Lightroom, **folders** should still be used to manage your physical image files on your computer. Lightroom tracks the location of your files within the folder structure, so keeping your files organized at the operating system level is just as important as organizing them within Lightroom.

SMART COLLECTIONS AND FILTERS

The combination of Smart Collections and filters is one of the most powerful aspects of Lightroom Classic 2025. These features allow you to automatically organize your images based on specific rules and quickly retrieve photos based on a variety of criteria.

Smart Collections

As mentioned earlier, Smart Collections are a game-changer for photographers with large catalogs. By creating rules based on keywords, metadata, flags, or ratings, you can set up collections that automatically update themselves whenever a new photo meets the criteria.

For example, you could create a Smart Collection for all photos that have a 4-star rating or higher, are flagged as picks, and have the keyword "landscape." Any time you import new images that meet those criteria, they will be added to the collection automatically. This saves time and ensures that your collection is always up to date.

Using Filters for Quick Organization

The **Filter Bar** is another essential tool in Lightroom Classic. It allows you to quickly sort and filter images based on flags, ratings, labels, metadata, and keywords. You can even combine multiple filters to narrow down your results further. For example, you could filter by images that are rated 5 stars, flagged as picks, and labeled with a specific color. This level of detail makes it easy to organize and find specific images quickly.

In this chapter, we've covered a wide range of tools and techniques that will help you organize and manage your photos in Lightroom Classic 2025. From importing and exporting images to rating, flagging, labeling, and using advanced photo organization features like collections and Smart Collections, you now have a solid understanding of how to efficiently handle your growing image library.

By applying these organizational strategies, you'll be able to work faster, more efficiently, and stay on top of your photo management. As you continue through the guide, you'll learn how to apply these organizational techniques to streamline your editing workflow, allowing you to focus more on creating stunning images and less on managing files.

CHAPTER 3: THE DEVELOP MODULE – EDITING BASICS

INTRODUCTION TO THE DEVELOP MODULE

Welcome to the heart of Lightroom Classic: the **Develop Module**. If the **Library Module** is where you organize and manage your photos, the **Develop Module** is where the magic happens. This is the space where you can take your raw images and turn them into stunning, polished works of art. Whether you're aiming for a clean, professional look or experimenting with dramatic edits, the Develop Module gives you complete control over how your photos appear.

At first glance, the Develop Module may seem a bit overwhelming. There are sliders, panels, and options everywhere, each offering a new way to adjust the image you've brought into Lightroom. But don't worry—this chapter will help demystify the interface and introduce you to the basic tools that are essential for effective photo editing. By the end of this chapter, you'll have a solid understanding of how to use the Develop Module to enhance your images, fine-tune exposure, apply color corrections, and use some of the more advanced tools that Lightroom offers.

The beauty of Lightroom Classic lies in its **non-destructive editing** approach. This means that any edits you make are stored separately from the original image, allowing you to experiment freely without ever permanently altering the original file. If you're ever unhappy with an edit, you can always reset it or undo it entirely, and the original photo remains intact.

While the Develop Module offers a vast array of tools, this chapter focuses on the basics—those foundational adjustments that every photographer needs to know in order to get started with editing. Once you're comfortable with these tools, you can explore more advanced techniques in later chapters. But for now, we'll walk through the core adjustments that make up the majority of photo edits.

The Develop Module is all about making your photos look their best, whether you're correcting exposure, improving colors, or adding creative effects. Understanding how to use these tools effectively is key to achieving professional-level results. Let's dive in and start working with these powerful features.

BASIC EDITING TOOLS: EXPOSURE, CONTRAST, AND CLARITY

When you first enter the Develop Module, you'll be greeted with a wide range of editing options. But the foundation of photo editing starts with a few simple adjustments that make a world of difference: **Exposure**, **Contrast**, and **Clarity**. These three basic tools are the first things you should reach for when enhancing an image. They can dramatically affect the mood, tone, and overall look of your photos, and learning how to use them will give you a strong grasp on editing in Lightroom Classic.

Exposure: Getting the Right Light

Exposure refers to the overall brightness of your photo. If your image is too dark (underexposed) or too light (overexposed), adjusting the exposure slider will help balance it out. The **Exposure** slider is located in the **Basic Panel** on the right side of the Develop Module. By moving the slider to the right, you increase the exposure, making the image brighter. Conversely, moving it to the left will darken the image.

It's important to understand that exposure is the first and most critical adjustment when working with raw images. Unlike JPEG files, which have baked-in adjustments, raw files capture all the information from the camera's sensor, including both the highlights and shadows. The Exposure slider allows you to adjust how much light is captured, compensating for underexposed or overexposed shots.

While adjusting exposure, be mindful of the **highlight** and **shadow** details. Overexposing an image might cause you to lose important detail in the brightest areas, while underexposing might cause shadowed areas to become too dark to recover. Lightroom Classic gives you the option to bring those details back, but it's best to find a balanced exposure in the first place.

Contrast: Adding Depth to Your Image

The **Contrast** slider controls the difference between the light and dark areas of your image. A higher contrast makes the bright areas of your photo brighter and the dark areas darker, adding a sense of depth and drama. On the other hand, reducing contrast will create a more flat, even look, which can be useful in certain styles, like soft portraits or overcast landscapes.

Adding contrast can help make an image "pop," especially if the photo feels a bit flat or washed out. In landscape photography, for example, increasing contrast can emphasize the richness of the sky and the texture of the land. In portrait photography, careful use of contrast can highlight facial features or textures in the clothing or hair.

It's crucial to strike a balance when adjusting contrast—too much contrast can lead to loss of detail in both shadows and highlights, while too little can make an image feel flat and lifeless.

Clarity: Enhancing Midtone Detail

The **Clarity** slider is a tool that affects the midtones of your image, adding more contrast and texture without impacting the highlights and shadows. Increasing the clarity will enhance textures, such as the details in skin, fabric, or landscapes, making the image appear sharper and more defined. It can add a sense of crispness to your image, often enhancing the visual appeal, especially in portraits or outdoor photography.

However, it's essential to use clarity subtly. Too much clarity can create unnatural halos around edges, particularly in portraiture, where it can make skin appear overly sharp and unnatural. When editing landscapes or architectural photos, you can be more liberal with the clarity slider to bring out details in clouds, mountains, or buildings.

If you find that increasing clarity makes the image too harsh, you can always adjust the **Dehaze** tool (a separate tool in the Develop module) to soften the effect without losing too much detail.

By mastering these basic editing tools—**Exposure**, **Contrast**, and **Clarity**—you'll have the foundation to start improving the quality of any image you import into Lightroom Classic.

UNDERSTANDING THE TONE CURVE FOR BETTER CONTROL

Once you've become familiar with the basic editing tools, the next level of control comes with the **Tone Curve**. This powerful tool allows you to adjust the tonal range of your image with precision. While the basic sliders in the Basic Panel are fantastic for quick fixes, the **Tone Curve** offers more advanced control over the light and dark areas of your image.

The Tone Curve is essentially a graph that represents the range of tones in your image, from the darkest shadows on the left to the brightest highlights on the right. By manipulating the curve, you can adjust how the tonal values are distributed across your image. The more you learn about the Tone Curve, the more flexibility you'll have in creating detailed, well-balanced images.

Using the Tone Curve

The Tone Curve is divided into four regions: shadows, darks, lights, and highlights. Each region controls a specific part of the tonal range:

- **Shadows**: The far left of the curve controls the darkest areas of the image. Adjusting the shadows will affect how dark or light the deep areas of the image are.

- **Darks**: Slightly to the right of the shadows, this part controls the darker midtones in the image, affecting the deep yet not completely black regions.

- **Lights**: The middle of the curve controls the lighter midtones. Adjusting the lights affects the brightness of your image without impacting the pure whites.

- **Highlights**: The far right of the curve controls the brightest parts of your image, influencing how the highlights appear.

Manipulating the Curve

To manipulate the curve, you can click on the line and drag it up or down. When you drag the curve upwards, you brighten that tonal range, while dragging it down darkens it. By creating gentle S-curves, you can add contrast to the image, making the highlights brighter and the shadows darker, which is often used to add depth and richness.

Practical Tips for Using the Tone Curve

- For a **vintage or matte look**, you can lower the shadows and raise the highlights slightly, creating a softer, less contrasty image.

- For **dramatic contrast**, creating a strong S-curve (by pulling down the shadows and lifting the highlights) can give your image a punchy, high-impact look.

- Use the Tone Curve to **recover highlight details** by subtly lowering the curve at the highlight end, which can bring back detail in overexposed areas.

The Tone Curve is a tool that offers a higher level of control over your image's tonal adjustments, making it a valuable tool in any photographer's editing workflow. Learning how to use it effectively will open up new possibilities in enhancing the dynamic range of your photos.

COLOR ADJUSTMENTS: WHITE BALANCE AND HSL PANEL

Color is one of the most critical aspects of photo editing. Whether you want to correct your image to reflect accurate colors or add a creative color tone to set the mood, Lightroom Classic provides several tools to help you achieve your desired effect. Two essential tools for adjusting color are **White Balance** and the **HSL Panel (Hue, Saturation, and Luminance)**.

White Balance: Correcting Color Temperature

The **White Balance** tool is used to ensure that the colors in your image appear natural. Light sources vary in color temperature, from the warm tones of a sunrise to the cool hues of an overcast sky. If the white balance is off, your photos can appear unnaturally warm or cool, making the colors look unrealistic.

In Lightroom Classic, the White Balance tool is located at the top of the **Basic Panel**. You'll see a drop-down menu with several preset options, including **Daylight**, **Cloudy**, **Tungsten**, **Fluorescent**, and more. These presets are designed to correct common lighting situations and quickly adjust the overall color temperature of your image.

If you're not satisfied with a preset, you can fine-tune the color temperature and tint manually using the **Temperature** and **Tint** sliders. The **Temperature** slider controls the warmth of the image—moving it to the left cools the image, while moving it to the right warms it up. The **Tint** slider adjusts the green-magenta balance. Using these sliders, you can achieve the perfect white balance for any lighting condition.

HSL Panel: Creative Color Control

For more advanced color adjustments, the **HSL (Hue, Saturation, and Luminance)** panel in Lightroom Classic gives you precise control over individual colors in your image. This is an excellent tool for fine-tuning specific hues, making colors pop, or even removing unwanted color casts.

- **Hue**: This slider allows you to shift the hue of specific colors. For example, you can change the color of the sky from blue to teal or make grass appear more yellow. The Hue panel is useful when you want to create creative color effects or correct color imbalances.

- **Saturation**: The **Saturation** slider controls the intensity of specific colors. Increasing the saturation makes colors more vibrant, while decreasing it makes them more muted or even desaturated to grayscale.

- **Luminance**: The **Luminance** slider controls the brightness of specific colors in the image. If you want to brighten the sky or darken the greens in a landscape, the Luminance panel is the tool to use.

By mastering the HSL panel, you can take full control of the colors in your image, whether you're adjusting for accurate color correction or pursuing a more artistic or stylized look.

APPLYING AND USING PRESETS FOR FASTER WORKFLOW

As you become more familiar with Lightroom Classic's editing tools, you'll likely find that certain adjustments work well for specific types of photos. One of the best ways to save time and maintain consistency across multiple images is by using **presets**. Presets are pre-defined adjustments that can be applied to your photos with a single click, instantly applying a set of edits that you have saved.

What Are Presets?

Presets are essentially a collection of editing settings that are applied to an image at once. You can create your own presets or download presets from other photographers or online marketplaces. Whether you're working with a batch of photos from the same shoot or looking to apply a specific look to your images, presets streamline the editing process.

In Lightroom Classic, the **Presets Panel** is located on the left side of the Develop Module. Here, you'll find a variety of default presets, including basic options like **Auto Tone**, **B/W**, and **Vignettes**. You can also create custom presets tailored to your style or workflow. For example, you might create a preset that automatically adjusts exposure, contrast, and clarity for landscape photos, or one that applies a specific color grading for portraits.

How to Create and Apply Presets

Creating a preset is simple. Once you've edited an image to your liking, go to the **Presets Panel** and click the + icon to create a new preset. Lightroom will ask you which settings you want to include in the preset—whether it's the basic adjustments, the tone curve, color settings, or any other edits you've made. After saving it, your preset will appear in the list and can be applied to other photos with a single click.

Applying a preset is just as easy. Simply select the image you want to edit and click on the preset you want to use. The preset will instantly apply all the adjustments you've saved, allowing you to move on to the next image quickly. This is a huge time-saver, especially when you're working with large batches of photos that require similar adjustments.

Presets are also helpful for maintaining consistency in your editing. For example, if you're working on a series of photos for a client or a project, applying the same preset ensures that all your images have a similar look and feel.

CROPPING AND STRAIGHTENING YOUR IMAGES

In addition to the basic exposure and color adjustments, one of the simplest yet most effective edits you can make to your photos is **cropping** and **straightening**. These two tools can drastically improve the composition of your images, helping you create balanced and visually appealing shots.

Cropping Your Images

The **Crop Tool** is located in the Develop Module, just below the Histogram. To crop your image, simply click the **Crop Overlay** tool, and a grid will appear on your photo. From here, you can click and drag the corners or edges to adjust the crop area.

The **Aspect Ratio** dropdown allows you to select a specific crop ratio (such as 4:5, 16:9, or custom ratios), which is especially useful when you're preparing images for specific platforms or prints. You can also rotate the crop grid to adjust the image's orientation.

Straightening Your Image

In addition to cropping, Lightroom Classic offers an easy-to-use tool for straightening tilted images. The **Straighten Tool** is located in the Crop Panel. To use it, simply click the **Auto** button, or draw a line along an element in the image (such as the horizon or a building) that should be horizontal or vertical. Lightroom will automatically straighten the image to make the line align properly.

Both cropping and straightening tools are essential for improving your photo composition. By removing unnecessary elements, adjusting the framing, or ensuring that your horizons are level, you can make your images look more polished and professional.

In this chapter, we've covered the essential tools that will help you unlock the full potential of the **Develop Module** in Lightroom Classic 2025. From adjusting the **Exposure**, **Contrast**, and **Clarity** to fine-tuning your colors with the **White Balance** and **HSL Panel**, you now have the foundation to start editing your photos with confidence.

Mastering the **Tone Curve**, **presets**, and tools like **cropping** and **straightening** will help elevate your images, allowing you to make your photos pop and stand out. These are just the basics, and as you grow more comfortable with Lightroom, you can experiment with advanced techniques to further refine your work.

Whether you're working on personal projects or client work, the tools in the Develop Module are designed to give you complete control over the final look of your images. As you continue to practice and experiment, you'll discover even more ways to customize your editing workflow and achieve professional-level results. Let's keep exploring these powerful tools as we move forward in mastering Lightroom Classic.

CHAPTER 4: MASTERING ADVANCED EDITING TECHNIQUES

USING THE GRADUATED FILTER AND RADIAL FILTER FOR SELECTIVE EDITS

When you start editing photos in Lightroom Classic 2025, you'll quickly realize that one of the most powerful aspects of the software is its ability to perform **selective adjustments**. Sometimes, you don't want to apply changes to the entire image, but rather to specific areas that need improvement. That's where the **Graduated Filter** and **Radial Filter** tools come in. These two filters allow you to apply adjustments to just a portion of your image, providing greater control over how light, color, and exposure are distributed across your photo.

Understanding the Graduated Filter

The **Graduated Filter** tool is designed for making gradual adjustments to specific areas of an image, typically used for landscapes, skies, and other situations where you want to make a smooth transition from one area to another. It's particularly effective for editing the sky, bringing out more detail in clouds, or balancing an image where the foreground and background have very different exposure levels.

To use the Graduated Filter, click on the **Graduated Filter** icon in the Develop Module or press the keyboard shortcut **M**. Then, click and drag over the area of your image where you want the effect to begin and end. The Graduated Filter works by applying changes across the image in a linear gradient. The area where you start dragging will be fully affected, and the area where you stop dragging will remain unaffected. This gradient can be adjusted for a softer or harder transition, depending on how sharp or subtle you want the effect to be.

For example, imagine you're editing a landscape photo with a bright sky and a darker foreground. Using the Graduated Filter, you can apply a **negative exposure** adjustment to the sky, darkening it slightly without affecting the rest of the photo. You can also apply a **positive exposure** to the foreground to brighten it up, all while ensuring the transition between the two is smooth and natural.

The Radial Filter: Focused Editing Made Easy

On the other hand, the **Radial Filter** allows for more focused, circular adjustments to specific areas of your image. It's perfect for drawing attention to certain elements of your photo, such as a subject in a portrait, or creating a vignette around the edges of an image to enhance the central focal point. The Radial Filter is similar to the Graduated Filter, but instead of a linear gradient, it applies a circular mask with a sharp outer edge and a softer inner area.

To use the Radial Filter, select the **Radial Filter** tool from the toolbar (or press **Shift + M**). After that, click and drag over the area where you want to apply the adjustment. You can resize the circle to suit the size of the subject or area you're working with, and you can also adjust the feathering (the softness of the edge) to create a smoother transition.

One of the most common uses of the Radial Filter is for portrait editing. For instance, you can use it to brighten a person's face without affecting the background, or enhance the catchlights in their eyes. By using the Radial Filter creatively, you can isolate certain parts of your image and adjust them independently from the rest, giving you control over the final look of the image.

Both the Graduated and Radial Filters are excellent tools for making **local adjustments** in Lightroom Classic. By using these tools effectively, you can add a professional touch to your edits, ensuring that the most important parts of your image are emphasized and enhanced while leaving the rest of the scene untouched.

INTRODUCTION TO THE ADJUSTMENT BRUSH FOR FINE-TUNING

If you want even more precision when editing specific areas of your image, the **Adjustment Brush** is your go-to tool. While the Graduated and Radial Filters are fantastic for broader, linear or circular adjustments, the Adjustment Brush allows for detailed, **brushstroke-style editing**. This tool is ideal for fine-tuning areas of your image that require subtle adjustments, such as retouching skin, enhancing shadows in specific areas, or brightening a subject's face in a portrait.

How to Use the Adjustment Brush

To access the **Adjustment Brush**, click on the **Adjustment Brush** tool in the Develop Module or press **K** on your keyboard. Once the tool is selected, you'll see a set of sliders similar to those found in the Basic Panel (such as **Exposure**, **Contrast**, **Clarity**, and **Saturation**). These sliders allow you to make changes to specific areas that you paint over with the brush. You can increase or decrease exposure, adjust the sharpness, tweak the color balance, or even add a vignette effect.

Using the **Adjustment Brush** involves "painting" over the area where you want to apply the changes. You can adjust the **brush size** and **feathering** (the softness of the brush's edges) to suit your needs. You can also choose between a **flow** and **density** setting, which controls how gradually the brush applies the effect and how strong it is.

For example, if you're editing a portrait and want to smooth out the skin, you can use the **Adjustment Brush** to paint over the skin areas and apply a slight **negative clarity** adjustment. This will soften the skin without affecting the rest of the image. You can also use it to **brighten the eyes** or add detail to the lips, giving your subjects a more polished and professional look.

Masking and Refining with the Adjustment Brush

One of the most valuable features of the **Adjustment Brush** is its ability to mask specific areas for editing. When you paint over an area, Lightroom automatically creates a mask, and you can fine-tune this mask by refining the edges. The **auto mask** feature in Lightroom helps to detect edges in your photo, ensuring that the adjustments only apply to the areas you want to edit. For instance, if you're brightening the face, the auto mask will help you avoid affecting the hair or background.

If you make a mistake while painting, you can switch to the **Erase** brush to remove areas from the mask, giving you full control over the areas you want to adjust.

The **Adjustment Brush** is incredibly versatile and gives you the freedom to edit individual areas with high precision. Whether you're fine-tuning details in a portrait, enhancing textures in a landscape, or correcting specific lighting problems, the Adjustment Brush is an essential tool in Lightroom Classic's editing arsenal.

WORKING WITH THE RANGE MASK FOR MORE CONTROL

When working with the Graduated Filter, Radial Filter, or the Adjustment Brush, sometimes you'll find that the tool's effect is a bit too broad or uneven for the image you're working on. This is where the **Range Mask** comes in. It adds an extra layer of control, allowing you to limit the effect of your adjustments to specific tonal or color ranges.

How the Range Mask Works

The **Range Mask** is available in all three local adjustment tools: the **Graduated Filter**, **Radial Filter**, and **Adjustment Brush**. It enables you to make your adjustments more targeted by limiting them to either **highlights**, **shadows**, or **color** ranges. This is useful when you want to apply a filter or brush stroke only to specific tonal ranges in the image, such as brightening the shadows without affecting the highlights or removing a color cast in a specific area.

For example, if you're editing a sunset scene and want to enhance the colors in the sky without affecting the darker foreground, you can use the **Range Mask** to limit the effect of the Graduated Filter to only the highlights or midtones. Similarly, you can use the **color Range Mask** to isolate a specific color (like the blue of the sky) and make adjustments only to that color range, leaving other colors untouched.

Practical Applications of the Range Mask

The **Range Mask** feature can be a game-changer when it comes to making precise adjustments. Some common uses include:

- **Enhancing Skies**: If you're working with a landscape where the sky is too dull or washed out, you can use the Graduated Filter to brighten the sky. By enabling the **Range Mask** and selecting the **Highlights** option, you can ensure that only the bright areas of the sky are affected, preventing any unwanted changes to the rest of the image.

- **Selective Color Correction**: If you want to adjust a specific color in your photo (like changing the hue of a red dress in a portrait), you can use the **Color Range Mask** to target only the red tones, leaving the rest of the image untouched. This can help achieve precise color grading without affecting other parts of your photo.

The **Range Mask** provides an additional layer of control, giving you the freedom to make sophisticated edits without worrying about accidentally altering areas that should remain unchanged.

ADVANCED COLOR GRADING TECHNIQUES

Color grading is one of the most impactful aspects of photo editing. It's the art of adjusting and enhancing the colors in an image to create a particular mood, atmosphere, or visual style. Lightroom Classic offers a range of tools to help you with **color grading**, from basic adjustments to more advanced techniques for controlling the entire color palette.

The Color Grading Panel

The **Color Grading** panel, introduced in Lightroom Classic 2021, provides a powerful set of tools to fine-tune your image's color balance. It allows you to control the **shadows**, **midtones**, and **highlights** separately, giving you the ability to create complex and customized color looks. Each of these tonal ranges has its own set of sliders for adjusting **hue**, **saturation**, and **luminance**, so you can adjust colors in specific parts of your image.

For example, you might want to apply a **cool blue tint** to the shadows for a moody look, while adding a warm **orange hue** to the highlights to simulate a sunset effect. The flexibility of the Color Grading panel means you can be as subtle or as bold as you like with your color adjustments.

Using Split Toning for Creative Effects

Split toning is another popular technique in color grading. It involves adding different colors to the shadows and highlights of your image to create a unique effect. For example, you can add a cool blue to the shadows and a warm gold to the highlights, creating a pleasing contrast that enhances the mood of the photo.

In Lightroom, **Split Toning** is now integrated into the **Color Grading** panel, where you can adjust the hue and saturation of both shadows and highlights independently. This is ideal for creating cinematic effects, retro looks, or enhancing the overall vibe of your image.

Color Grading for Mood and Style

Advanced color grading techniques can be used to convey mood and emotion. For example, a warm color grade with golden tones can evoke a sense of warmth and comfort, while cool blues can create a more somber, mysterious feeling. When color grading your images, think about the emotional response you want to elicit from your viewers and use the tools at your disposal to enhance that effect.

USING THE TONE CURVE FOR PRECISION CONTROL

We covered the basics of the **Tone Curve** in Chapter 3, but this powerful tool deserves a deeper dive. The Tone Curve is one of the most versatile tools in Lightroom Classic for controlling exposure, contrast, and tonal balance with **precision**. By learning how to use the Tone Curve for advanced edits, you can make nuanced adjustments that would be difficult to achieve using the Basic Panel sliders alone.

Precision Adjustments with the Tone Curve

The Tone Curve lets you fine-tune the tonal range of your image, from the shadows to the highlights. Using the curve, you can adjust the **brightness** of specific areas with pinpoint accuracy. By clicking on the curve, you can create anchor points and drag them to modify the image's tonal distribution.

One advanced technique is to create an **S-curve**, where you lower the shadows and raise the highlights to increase the contrast of your image. This technique is commonly used in **portrait photography** to add depth and vibrance to skin tones, as well as in **landscape photography** to bring out the texture and detail in clouds and terrain.

HOW TO ACHIEVE STUNNING BLACK AND WHITE CONVERSIONS

While color editing is often the focus, sometimes the best way to bring out the beauty of an image is by removing color entirely. **Black and white conversion** is an art form in itself, and Lightroom Classic offers a wide range of tools to help you create stunning monochrome images.

Converting to Black and White

In Lightroom, converting a color image to black and white is simple. In the **Basic Panel**, you'll find the **Black & White** checkbox. Once you check this box, your image will automatically convert to grayscale. However, this is just the starting point, and there are several advanced techniques you can use to refine the look and feel of your black-and-white images.

Using the HSL Panel for Black and White Conversion

Even in black and white, color still plays an important role. Lightroom allows you to manipulate the **luminosity** of specific colors during the conversion process. This means you can adjust how light or dark certain colors appear in the final black-and-white image. For example, you might want the sky (which may be blue in color) to appear darker, or the skin tones to be brighter. The HSL (Hue, Saturation, Luminance) panel is perfect for this kind of fine-tuning.

By adjusting the luminance of specific colors, you can control the tonal range of your image and create more dramatic, visually engaging black-and-white photos.

Mastering advanced editing techniques in Lightroom Classic 2025 opens up a world of creative possibilities. By learning how to use the **Graduated and Radial Filters**, **Adjustment Brush**, **Range Mask**, and advanced **color grading** techniques, you can elevate your photography and take full control of your images. Each of these tools provides unique ways to enhance your photos with precision and creativity, making them essential in any photographer's editing toolkit.

With practice and experimentation, you'll find that these advanced techniques become second nature, allowing you to edit with ease and confidence. As you continue to work with Lightroom Classic, these tools will empower you to create professional-level edits that bring your vision to life. Whether you're fine-tuning the smallest details or transforming an entire image, these techniques will help you achieve the stunning results you've always envisioned.

CHAPTER 5: ADVANCED RETOUCHING AND IMAGE RESTORATION

SPOT REMOVAL AND HEALING TOOLS FOR FLAWLESS IMAGES

Retouching is often the secret behind a professional-looking image. It's the art of improving the aesthetic quality of your photo without completely changing its essence. When we talk about retouching in Lightroom Classic 2025, one of the most vital tools you'll use is the **Spot Removal** tool. Whether you're dealing with dust spots from your lens, blemishes on a portrait, or any unwanted distractions in the background, this tool offers an easy and efficient solution for removing imperfections while preserving the integrity of the image.

The Spot Removal Tool: Understanding the Basics

The **Spot Removal** tool is located in the Develop module, and it's primarily used to remove small spots, distractions, or imperfections from your image. You can access it by either clicking the **Spot Removal** icon or pressing the **Q** key on your keyboard. Once activated, you will see a circular brush appear on your image. This circle represents the area Lightroom will correct, and you can resize the brush to fit the area you're working on. You simply click on the spot or imperfection you want to remove, and Lightroom will automatically attempt to find a suitable area from which to copy pixels, effectively "healing" the issue.

What makes the **Spot Removal** tool powerful is its ability to blend the surrounding areas seamlessly. It's not just about erasing an imperfection, but about filling it with texture, color, and light that match the surrounding parts of the image. This creates a natural look, so your edit doesn't feel artificial.

Using the Healing Brush for More Complex Edits

While the Spot Removal tool is excellent for quick fixes, some situations require more finesse, especially when you're dealing with more complex textures or gradients. This is where the **Healing Brush** comes into play. The Healing Brush works similarly to the Spot Removal tool but offers more control over the way the tool samples surrounding areas.

To use the **Healing Brush**, you select the tool in the same way as the Spot Removal tool, but with the difference that Lightroom now allows you to manually control the sampling process. Instead of relying entirely on Lightroom to find a similar area, you can select the area you want to use as a sample for the healing process, giving you greater flexibility and control.

The Difference Between Clone and Heal Modes

When using the Spot Removal tool, Lightroom gives you two modes to work with: **Clone** and **Heal**. Understanding the difference between these modes is key to achieving flawless edits:

- **Clone**: This mode simply duplicates pixels from one part of your image and places them over the problem area. The Clone tool is ideal for situations where the surrounding area is relatively uniform, such as a clear sky or an even surface like a wall.

- **Heal**: This mode works by blending the surrounding area with the problem spot, ensuring a smoother transition and more natural-looking results. Heal is especially useful for skin retouching and areas with texture, like grass or fabric, where the result needs to match the surrounding environment seamlessly.

You can easily toggle between these modes by selecting the appropriate option in the tool settings, allowing you to tailor the solution based on the complexity of your image.

Practical Applications for Spot Removal and Healing Tools

Spot removal and healing tools are most often used in portrait photography to remove blemishes, scars, and imperfections in the skin. However, these tools are just as effective in landscape photography for removing dust spots caused by the lens, or for eliminating distracting elements like trash or unwanted signs.

For example, in a landscape photo, if you see a stray leaf or piece of debris in the frame that detracts from the image's aesthetic, you can use the **Spot Removal** tool to remove it. Similarly, in a portrait, if a model has a small blemish or stray hair, these tools allow you to fix the issue without the need for Photoshop.

USING THE CLONE TOOL FOR PRECISION EDITING

While the **Spot Removal** and **Healing** tools are great for most minor edits, there are instances when you need to go a step further and perform more **precision editing**. This is where the **Clone Tool** in Lightroom Classic 2025 becomes invaluable. Unlike the Spot Removal tool, which is often used for small blemishes or imperfections, the **Clone Tool** is designed for larger areas where you need to replicate a section of your image.

Understanding the Clone Tool

The Clone Tool in Lightroom is primarily used for larger, more complex tasks. It works by copying pixels from one part of the image and placing them over another area. The Clone tool is especially useful when you need to remove a large object, like a distracting building in a landscape or an unwanted shadow in a portrait.

Using the Clone Tool involves selecting a source area, much like the Spot Removal tool, but the tool allows you to more deliberately control the pixel source for cloning. You can pick any area in the photo that matches the section you want to cover, and the Clone tool will take care of the rest, making the transition as smooth as possible.

Precision with the Clone Tool

What sets the Clone Tool apart is its ability to provide more control and precision. For example, if you're removing a large object from an image, such as a streetlight or signpost, you can select a source that closely matches the area you want to hide, and Lightroom will copy that area and paste it over the unwanted object.

However, while the Clone Tool provides more flexibility than the Spot Removal tool, it still requires a keen eye for detail. If you don't choose a proper source area, the results may look artificial or jarring. It's important to pick your source wisely, ensuring that it matches the texture, color, and light conditions of the area you're trying to cover.

Practical Applications for the Clone Tool

The Clone Tool is invaluable for situations where you need to remove objects that are too large or complex for the Spot Removal tool. In landscape photography, this could mean removing a distracting tree branch, a power line, or any other object that disrupts the composition of the shot. In portrait photography, the Clone Tool can be used to remove distractions in the background or fix larger skin imperfections that require precise adjustments.

REDUCING NOISE AND SHARPENING YOUR IMAGES

One of the most challenging aspects of photo editing, particularly with images shot in low light or at high ISO settings, is managing **noise**. Noise can appear as random color speckles or grain in your photos, often detracting from the clarity and smoothness you're trying to achieve. Fortunately, Lightroom Classic offers robust tools for **noise reduction** and **sharpening**, both of which are essential for achieving professional-level images.

Noise Reduction: What You Need to Know

Noise typically appears in the darker areas of an image, particularly in low-light shots. It's especially prominent when shooting with higher ISO settings, as the camera amplifies the signal to make the image brighter, which also amplifies any noise present. While some noise is inevitable, Lightroom offers powerful tools to help reduce it.

In Lightroom Classic, the **Noise Reduction** sliders are located in the **Detail Panel**. These sliders help you manage both **Luminance** (the brightness of the noise) and **Color** (the color of the noise). The **Luminance** slider helps smooth out the grainy appearance without sacrificing too much detail, while the **Color** slider removes color noise, which often manifests as unwanted random hues in your shadows.

While Lightroom's noise reduction tools are effective, they can sometimes soften the image, leading to a loss of detail. This is why it's essential to find a balance between reducing noise and maintaining sharpness.

Sharpening Your Image

After reducing noise, it's often necessary to apply **sharpening** to bring back the crispness and detail in your image. The **Sharpening** slider in the **Detail Panel** controls how sharp your image appears by enhancing the edges in your photo. Lightroom applies sharpening through a process known as **unsharp masking**, which enhances the contrast along edges to create the illusion of sharpness.

Sharpening is a delicate process because over-sharpening can introduce artifacts like halos and noise. It's crucial to fine-tune the sharpening settings, particularly the **Radius** and **Detail** sliders, to ensure that you're enhancing the fine details without making the image look unnatural.

Practical Applications for Noise Reduction and Sharpening

Noise reduction is especially useful for images shot in low light or with high ISO, such as night photography or indoor shots. Sharpening is useful in almost every photo, but it's particularly important for landscape images or when you need to highlight fine details, such as textures in clothing or scenery.

WORKING WITH THE DEHAZE TOOL

The **Dehaze Tool** is a unique and powerful feature in Lightroom Classic that allows you to remove or add haze in your images. Whether you're working with foggy landscapes, misty cityscapes, or shots taken under overcast skies, this tool helps you bring back lost clarity and contrast.

How the Dehaze Tool Works

The Dehaze slider is found in the **Develop Module**, just below the **Basic Panel**. By moving the slider to the right, you can **remove haze** from your image, increasing contrast and bringing out details that may have been obscured by atmospheric conditions. Moving the slider to the left adds haze, which can be useful if you're going for a dreamy, atmospheric effect.

The **Dehaze Tool** works by targeting midtones and shadows, enhancing contrast and clarity in areas that are often affected by fog, mist, or smoke. It works particularly well in landscape photography, where distant mountains or objects often appear washed out due to atmospheric haze.

Practical Uses for the Dehaze Tool

The Dehaze tool is perfect for improving the visibility of distant elements, especially in wide-angle landscape shots. It's also effective in post-processing photos taken in hazy conditions, such as foggy mornings, where the atmosphere distorts the clarity of the image.

SKIN RETOUCHING AND PORTRAIT EDITING TECHNIQUES

Portraiture is an art in itself, and the tools provided by Lightroom Classic 2025 allow for detailed **skin retouching** and editing that can transform a good portrait into a stunning one. While Lightroom may not have the extensive tools available in Photoshop, its **local adjustment** features—such as the **Adjustment Brush** and **Radial Filter**—make it possible to achieve beautiful, subtle portrait edits directly within Lightroom.

Basic Skin Retouching Techniques

The first step in portrait editing is often **skin smoothing**. Lightroom offers tools like the **Adjustment Brush** that allow you to adjust the **clarity** of the skin without affecting the entire image. You can reduce **clarity** to soften the skin while avoiding overly smoothing out important texture details, like hair and eyes.

Another important aspect of portrait editing is the **highlighting** of the eyes and **enhancing facial features**. You can use the **Adjustment Brush** to add exposure to the eyes or lighten the teeth for a cleaner look, all while maintaining a natural feel.

Color Grading for Portraits

For portraits, color grading plays a significant role in setting the mood. Subtle use of the **HSL panel** can help adjust the skin tones, bringing out a healthy, natural color or creating a more stylized look. Additionally, the **Radial Filter** can be used to selectively brighten the face or other key features, making the subject stand out from the background.

Advanced retouching and image restoration in Lightroom Classic 2025 offer a wealth of powerful tools to help photographers enhance their images. Whether you're using the **Spot Removal** and **Healing Tools** for flawless skin, the **Clone Tool** for precision edits, or the **Dehaze Tool** to restore clarity, Lightroom gives you complete control over your editing process. By mastering these tools, you'll be able to take your photo editing skills to the next level, transforming everyday shots into extraordinary works of art.

CHAPTER 6: MASTERING MASKING IN LIGHTROOM CLASSIC

INTRODUCTION TO MASKING TECHNIQUES

One of the most powerful editing tools available in Adobe Lightroom Classic 2025 is **masking**. If you're a photographer, you know that sometimes a photo needs more than just global adjustments to look its best. Often, certain areas of an image require fine-tuned edits while leaving the rest of the photo unchanged. This is where masking comes in. Masking allows you to apply specific adjustments to selected parts of your image, giving you greater creative control and precision. Whether you're brightening up a subject's face, enhancing the sky, or sharpening a small detail, **masking** is the technique you'll turn to for fine-grained adjustments.

While Lightroom has always been known for its user-friendly interface and powerful non-destructive editing, masking techniques have traditionally been a bit limited. However, with the release of Lightroom Classic 2025, Adobe has introduced a **new generation of masking tools**, making them more powerful, accurate, and versatile than ever before. Now, you can achieve complex edits and adjustments with ease—without the need for additional software or advanced skills.

Masking isn't just about fixing mistakes; it's about **enhancing** your creativity and achieving professional-level results. Whether you're working on a portrait, landscape, or product photography, mastering masking will allow you to make more precise and tailored adjustments to your photos. The real magic happens when you learn how to use these tools effectively, enabling you to transform an ordinary shot into something truly special.

In this chapter, we'll dive deep into the **masking techniques** that will elevate your photo editing skills. We'll explore everything from basic selections to advanced options, helping you understand when and how to use these tools for maximum effect. By the end of this chapter, you'll be equipped with the knowledge to manipulate any part of your image, giving you the freedom to create flawless photos with a polished finish.

But before we get into the specifics of the latest masking tools, it's essential to understand the **fundamentals of masking**—the basic principles that will form the foundation of all your future edits. Whether you're new to masking or already have some experience, this chapter will provide a thorough guide on how to incorporate these techniques into your Lightroom workflow.

CREATING AND REFINING MASKS IN LIGHTROOM

At its core, **masking** is all about creating a selection that lets you apply edits to a specific part of your image, while leaving the rest untouched. But how do you create and refine those masks? In Lightroom Classic 2025, this process has been made intuitive, allowing you to work with several methods of selection—each offering different degrees of control. Let's take a closer look at how to create and refine masks in Lightroom.

Creating Basic Masks

Lightroom Classic provides several tools for creating masks, from **simple brush strokes** to **geometric shapes** that define the area for your edits. To get started with a basic mask, you'll need to head over to the **Develop Module**. Here, you'll see the **Masking** panel, which houses the tools you'll use to define your selection.

To create a mask using the **Adjustment Brush**, simply click on the **Brush Masking Tool**. You can then paint over areas of the image where you want to apply adjustments. The **brush size**, **feathering**, and **flow** are all adjustable, giving you total control over the mask's edges and the intensity of the effect. For example, if you're retouching a portrait, you can use a **soft brush** with **low flow** to gently paint over the skin, blending adjustments seamlessly.

Refining Masks for Precision

Once you've created a basic mask, you'll often need to refine it. This is where Lightroom's intuitive masking options really shine. Refining your mask is about making sure that it's applied exactly where you want it, without spilling over into areas that should remain untouched.

There are several ways to refine your mask:

- **Feathering**: This option softens the edges of your mask, creating a smooth transition between the selected and unselected areas. Feathering is essential for natural-looking adjustments, especially when you're working with portraits or landscapes where hard lines would look unnatural.

- **Inverting the Mask**: Sometimes, you might want to apply your adjustments to the opposite part of the image. You can do this by simply **inverting** the mask, which swaps the selected and unselected areas.

- **Refine Edge Brush**: One of Lightroom's recent additions, the **Refine Edge Brush**, helps you easily clean up edges where your mask may have unintentionally spilled over. You can use this brush to quickly remove any unwanted areas of the mask or adjust fine details in areas that need more precision.

Using the Mask Overlay for Visual Guidance

As you work with masks, it's easy to lose track of where you've painted or selected. To help you see exactly where your mask is applied, Lightroom Classic includes a **Mask Overlay** feature. When enabled, this tool will show you a **red or transparent overlay** wherever you've applied a mask. This visual guide is a real time-saver, especially when working with complex images or multiple masks.

USING THE NEW MASKING TOOLS IN LIGHTROOM CLASSIC 2025

Lightroom Classic 2025 introduced a host of exciting new **masking tools**, revolutionizing how photographers approach local adjustments. While the **Adjustment Brush** has been a staple for years, the new **AI-powered masking tools** allow you to make even more sophisticated selections with a few clicks. Let's dive into the new tools and how they can enhance your editing experience.

The AI Masking Tools: Select Subject and Select Sky

Two of the most notable additions to the masking toolbox are **Select Subject** and **Select Sky**, both powered by Adobe's **AI technology**. These tools are designed to automatically identify specific elements in your photo, making it easier to create masks without manual selection.

- **Select Subject**: This tool automatically detects and creates a mask around the main subject of the image. Whether it's a person, animal, or object, Lightroom Classic's AI will quickly identify and select it for you, saving you time and effort compared to manual brushing or creating complex selections. Once the subject is selected, you can apply any adjustments to enhance it—whether that's sharpening the details, adjusting exposure, or applying creative color grading.

- **Select Sky**: As the name suggests, this tool targets the sky in your image, making it incredibly useful for landscape photography. If you've ever tried to adjust the sky in a landscape image manually, you know how challenging it can be to avoid affecting the ground. With **Select Sky**, Lightroom does the heavy lifting by identifying the sky and creating a mask around it, allowing you to easily adjust colors, exposure, or contrast in the sky alone.

How to Use the New AI Tools

To use these tools, simply click on the **Masking** panel and choose either **Select Subject** or **Select Sky**. Lightroom will automatically generate a mask based on your selection, and you can refine it further if necessary. For instance, if Lightroom detects some unwanted elements in the mask (like tree branches in the sky), you can use the **brush** tool to fine-tune the selection.

These AI tools offer unparalleled speed and accuracy, especially when working with complex images or large batches of photos. They allow you to focus more on your creative vision and less on the tedious task of manual selection.

COLOR AND LUMINANCE MASKING FOR PRECISION CONTROL

When it comes to achieving precise edits in Lightroom Classic, **Color Masking** and **Luminance Masking** are invaluable tools. These tools allow you to make adjustments based on specific colors or tonal ranges in your image, providing you with a level of control that is difficult to achieve with basic brushes or filters alone.

Color Masking: Targeting Specific Colors

Color Masking lets you target specific colors in your image and make adjustments exclusively to those areas. This is particularly useful for enhancing or correcting individual colors, such as making a blue sky more vibrant, tweaking skin tones in a portrait, or adjusting the greens in a landscape.

To use Color Masking, click on the **Masking** panel and select **Color Range**. You can then use the color picker to sample a color from the image. Lightroom will automatically select areas that match that color, and you can apply adjustments such as saturation, exposure, or contrast to those areas only.

For example, if you want to make the grass in a landscape shot more vibrant, you can use Color Masking to select the green tones and then boost their saturation or exposure. This gives you total control over the color palette in your image.

Luminance Masking: Working with Brightness Levels

Luminance Masking allows you to create a mask based on the brightness or darkness of specific areas in your image. This tool is ideal when you want to adjust highlights or shadows without affecting midtones or other parts of the image.

To use Luminance Masking, select **Luminance Range** from the Masking panel. Lightroom will then allow you to define which brightness levels you want to target, from dark shadows to bright highlights. You can fine-tune the range by adjusting the sliders to narrow or broaden the mask, ensuring that it affects only the areas you want.

For instance, you could use **Luminance Masking** to brighten a dark foreground without affecting the bright sky. Similarly, you can darken the sky in a sunset photo while leaving the rest of the image untouched, which would be much harder to achieve without this tool.

Practical Applications of Color and Luminance Masking

These two techniques are incredibly powerful when you need to focus on specific parts of the image that require subtle adjustments. You can combine them to create even more complex edits. For instance, you can use **Color Masking** to enhance the blues of the ocean and **Luminance Masking** to adjust the highlights of the waves, creating a vibrant, eye-catching image with perfect tonal balance.

BRUSH MASKING VS. GRADIENT MASKING: WHEN TO USE EACH

At this point, you've learned about various methods of masking, including **Brush Masking, Gradient Masking**, and AI-driven tools. But when should you use each of these? Understanding when and why to use Brush or Gradient masking will improve your workflow and lead to more efficient edits.

Brush Masking: Fine-Tuning Details

The **Brush Masking** tool is your go-to option when you need precision. It allows you to paint over specific areas of your image with complete control, making it perfect for detailed work such as **retouching** a subject's face, adjusting the brightness of a specific object, or fixing small flaws.

When to use it: Use Brush Masking when the area you want to adjust is irregular or complex, like skin in a portrait, small details in a landscape, or any other area that requires specific attention.

Gradient Masking: Smooth Transitions

Gradient Masking is ideal when you need a gradual, smooth transition between adjusted and non-adjusted areas. It's commonly used for landscape photography, such as brightening the foreground or darkening the sky with a smooth, even effect. Gradient masks are also great for situations where you want a more natural-looking fade between the edited and unedited parts of your photo.

When to use it: Use **Gradient Masking** when working with landscapes, skies, or any other areas where you need to apply adjustments gradually. It's perfect for evenly blending effects over a larger portion of an image.

Mastering **masking** techniques is essential for unlocking the full creative potential of Lightroom Classic 2025. Whether you're using **brush masking** for fine details, **gradient masking** for smoother transitions, or the latest **AI-powered tools** for quick and accurate selections, these tools provide the precision and control you need to elevate your photo editing.

By practicing these techniques, you'll be able to make selective adjustments with ease, enhancing the areas of your images that matter most while leaving the rest untouched. With the new masking features in Lightroom Classic 2025, the possibilities for creative expression are endless, and the more you experiment, the more confident you'll become in your ability to perfect your images.

As you continue to refine your workflow and experiment with masking techniques, you'll find that your images not only become more polished but also more dynamic, with every adjustment tailored to your unique vision.

CHAPTER 7: ADVANCED WORKFLOW AND EFFICIENCY TIPS

SETTING UP YOUR LIGHTROOM PREFERENCES FOR MAXIMUM SPEED

In the world of digital photography, time is a precious resource. Whether you're editing a single photo or processing hundreds from a recent shoot, efficiency can make or break your workflow. One of the best ways to streamline your Lightroom Classic experience is by **setting up your preferences**. Lightroom Classic 2025 offers a range of preferences that can dramatically improve your editing speed, performance, and overall productivity. By tailoring the software to your specific needs, you'll be able to save valuable time and focus more on your creative process.

Navigating Lightroom Preferences

When you first open Lightroom Classic 2025, you'll find a wide variety of default settings that Adobe has configured for general use. However, **Lightroom's Preferences** menu is where you'll find options to personalize the software for your unique workflow. To access Preferences, simply go to the **Edit** menu on Windows or the **Lightroom** menu on Mac, and select **Preferences**.

In the Preferences panel, there are multiple tabs, each of which governs a specific aspect of Lightroom's performance and behavior. From here, you can adjust settings related to **general appearance**, **performance**, **file handling**, and more. While it may seem like a lot to take in at first, optimizing your preferences can lead to faster load times, smoother editing, and less frustration as you work.

Maximizing Performance with Lightroom Preferences

One of the most impactful areas to adjust for maximum speed is the **Performance** tab in Lightroom's Preferences menu. Here, Lightroom lets you allocate system resources to improve speed and responsiveness. For example, you can increase the amount of **graphics processor (GPU) acceleration** that Lightroom uses. Enabling GPU acceleration speeds up tasks such as adjusting the develop sliders, zooming into images, and working with large files. For users with a more powerful system, enabling this option can significantly improve Lightroom's overall responsiveness.

You should also take a look at the **Camera Raw Cache** settings. Lightroom stores a cache of previews from your raw images, so when you re-open a photo, it doesn't need to reload everything from scratch. By increasing the **Cache Size** (typically 5-10 GB or more, depending on your storage capacity), Lightroom can keep a larger buffer of images on hand, speeding up your workflow and reducing lag.

File Handling and Import Settings

Another key aspect of your workflow involves how Lightroom handles your files. Within the **File Handling** tab, you'll find options for controlling **previews**, **import settings**, and **metadata options**. Setting your import preferences to automatically apply **basic edits** or **metadata** during the import process can save you time later, reducing the number of adjustments you need to make when you begin editing.

For example, if you regularly apply a particular **exposure** or **white balance** setting for your images, you can configure Lightroom to automatically apply a preset upon import. Similarly, Lightroom allows you to apply **metadata** and **keywords** on import, meaning your images will be organized and searchable immediately.

Customization for Efficiency

Lastly, make sure to adjust the **interface** preferences to suit your editing style. Lightroom Classic allows you to hide certain panels or tweak the size of others, helping you focus only on the tools you use most often. You can also change the **keyboard shortcuts** to suit your workflow, giving you quicker access to the tools you need most.

By setting up your Lightroom preferences correctly, you not only make the software more responsive but also tailor it to your own needs and editing habits. Over time, these small adjustments can add up to significant improvements in speed, ultimately giving you more time to focus on your creative work.

EFFICIENT FILE MANAGEMENT AND BACKUP STRATEGIES

Once you've adjusted your preferences for maximum performance, the next step in streamlining your Lightroom Classic workflow is developing an efficient **file management** and **backup strategy**. Proper file management not only ensures that your photos are organized, but it also makes it easier to find the images you need when you need them. Coupled with a solid backup plan, you can safeguard your valuable work and keep everything running smoothly.

The Importance of a Structured Folder System

One of the first steps in organizing your files is creating a **structured folder system** on your computer or external drive. This system will form the foundation for managing your Lightroom catalog and images effectively. It's essential to choose a consistent naming convention and folder hierarchy that works for your specific workflow. For example, you could organize your photos by **shoot date**, **client name**, or **project**.

In Lightroom, the images themselves live in folders on your computer, and Lightroom keeps track of their location in the **catalog**. Therefore, creating a folder structure from the start helps Lightroom maintain an organized system, making it easy to find, access, and manage your photos. The key to a successful folder system is to make it logical and scalable, especially if you're working with large amounts of data. For example, within each year's folder, you can create subfolders for individual shoots or projects, ensuring everything stays neat and accessible.

Catalog Management

In Lightroom, the catalog serves as the central database for all your images and edits. It's critical that your catalog is properly managed to avoid issues like **slow performance** or **file corruption**. Always keep your catalog in a dedicated folder, separate from your image files, and ensure it's regularly backed up.

It's also important to organize your catalog effectively. You can create **collections** to group photos based on specific projects, themes, or clients, making it easier to locate images later on. Use **smart collections** to automate the process by automatically grouping photos based on specific criteria, like star ratings, flags, or keywords.

Backup Strategies for Lightroom

Backing up your photos and catalog is crucial. Hard drives can fail, and external storage can be compromised, so it's always best to have a **redundant backup** plan in place. Lightroom offers an automatic **catalog backup feature**, which you can set up to create regular backups of your catalog file. However, this backup should not be your only safeguard.

In addition to Lightroom's catalog backup, make it a habit to back up your entire photo library and catalog to a **cloud storage service** or an external hard drive. Consider using a **RAID** (Redundant Array of Independent Disks) system for an extra layer of protection, as this type of storage automatically mirrors your data onto multiple drives.

By implementing a solid backup strategy and organizing your file system effectively, you can rest assured that your work is safe and well-structured, allowing you to focus on the creative aspects of your workflow without worrying about losing important data.

USING VIRTUAL COPIES TO EXPERIMENT WITHOUT LOSING ORIGINAL SHOTS

One of Lightroom's most powerful features is the ability to create **Virtual Copies**. As a photographer, you might find yourself editing the same image in multiple ways—trying different looks, experimenting with various presets, or testing alternative crops. Normally, making such changes would require creating multiple copies of the same file, which can quickly take up valuable storage space. However, with **Virtual Copies**, Lightroom allows you to experiment with different edits without actually duplicating the original file.

What Are Virtual Copies?

A **Virtual Copy** is a reference to the original file in your catalog, but with a separate set of adjustments and edits applied to it. Essentially, it's a way to create an "alternate version" of an image without duplicating the file itself. Virtual Copies don't take up extra disk space because they don't store a separate file; instead, they record the unique edits in your Lightroom catalog.

To create a Virtual Copy, simply right-click on the image in the Library or Develop module and select **Create Virtual Copy**. Lightroom will create a duplicate entry in your catalog, but only the adjustments will be different between the two versions. You can edit one Virtual Copy with a different preset or crop, while leaving the original untouched.

Benefits of Using Virtual Copies

The main benefit of Virtual Copies is that they let you experiment freely. For example, if you want to apply different processing styles (such as a high-contrast look versus a more muted one), you can create two Virtual Copies of the same image. These copies can have completely different edits without creating unnecessary physical duplicates of the image.

Virtual Copies are also great for **comparing images** side by side. You can work on one version and use the other as a reference, ensuring that you're always staying on track with your creative vision. Once you've decided on the final version, you can delete the Virtual Copies you no longer need, saving space in your catalog and system.

Practical Applications for Virtual Copies

Virtual Copies are especially useful when editing large batches of photos or when experimenting with creative edits. For example, you can create a Virtual Copy of a portrait to experiment with different retouching methods, or try different crops of a landscape shot. The flexibility and efficiency of Virtual Copies allow you to explore all your editing options without the fear of losing your original shot.

SYNCHRONIZING SETTINGS ACROSS MULTIPLE IMAGES

When working on a large set of photos, such as a wedding shoot or a product catalog, you'll often find that certain edits—like exposure adjustments, white balance corrections, or color grading—should be applied to multiple images. Lightroom makes this process easy with the **Synchronize** function, which allows you to apply your settings to all selected images with a single click.

How to Use Synchronization in Lightroom

To synchronize settings across multiple images, start by selecting the image you've edited in the Develop module. Then, hold down the **Shift** or **Ctrl** (Windows) / **Cmd** (Mac) key and click on the other images you'd like to adjust. With the images selected, click the **Sync** button in the bottom right corner of the Develop module. Lightroom will then apply the adjustments made to the selected photo to all the others, saving you time and effort.

You can choose which settings you want to synchronize by clicking the **Check All** or **Check None** button in the Synchronize dialog box. You can also individually select which adjustments to sync, such as exposure, tone curve, or even specific brushes or gradients.

Why Synchronization Is Important

Synchronization is a huge time-saver when editing large batches of photos. For example, if you've edited the first photo of a group of similar images, you don't have to manually adjust every single one. Instead, you can synchronize the settings to all the other images, ensuring a consistent look across the entire shoot.

By using synchronization effectively, you'll save hours of editing time, and ensure that your photos maintain uniformity in exposure, white balance, and overall style.

BATCH EDITING: HOW TO SAVE TIME WITH PRESETS AND SYNCING

When you have a large number of images to edit, batch editing is a crucial part of maintaining efficiency. Lightroom Classic 2025 offers several features that allow you to apply settings to multiple images at once, saving time and effort while ensuring consistency across your images. Using **presets** and **syncing** features together, you can quickly apply your preferred settings to an entire group of images.

Using Presets for Batch Editing

Lightroom's **Presets** are an excellent tool for batch editing. By creating custom presets for your most common adjustments—such as exposure, contrast, clarity, or color grading—you can apply these settings to multiple images in a single step. You can create **user-defined presets** for different types of edits, like a preset for landscapes or portraits, and then apply it to the entire batch.

To apply a preset to multiple images, select the photos you want to edit, go to the **Develop** module, and click on the desired preset from the **Presets Panel**. Lightroom will automatically apply the preset's settings to all the selected images, ensuring that they all have a consistent look.

Batch Editing with Syncing

In addition to using presets, Lightroom's **Sync** function allows you to apply edits made on one image to a group of selected images. As discussed earlier, you can select the image you've edited and then synchronize it to other photos by using the **Sync Settings** button.

By combining **presets** and **syncing**, you can dramatically speed up your workflow and ensure consistency across a large batch of photos. This is especially helpful when working with similar images, such as shots from the same event or product shots in a series.

Efficient workflow and time-saving techniques are essential for professional photographers who want to stay organized and productive. In this chapter, we explored the advanced features of Lightroom Classic 2025 that can help you work smarter, not harder. By setting up your preferences for optimal performance, creating a solid file management and backup strategy, using Virtual Copies, and mastering synchronization and batch editing, you can significantly reduce the time spent on repetitive tasks.

With these tools at your disposal, you can devote more time to the creative aspects of your work, knowing that your workflow is streamlined and efficient. As you continue to use Lightroom Classic, these techniques will become second nature, helping you maintain a fast, organized, and productive editing environment.

CHAPTER 8: INTEGRATING LIGHTROOM WITH OTHER ADOBE TOOLS

USING LIGHTROOM WITH PHOTOSHOP FOR ADVANCED EDITING

In the world of professional photo editing, there are very few combinations that rival the power and versatility of Adobe Lightroom and Adobe Photoshop. While Lightroom Classic 2025 is an exceptional tool for organizing, editing, and managing large batches of images, **Photoshop** brings advanced editing capabilities that push your creative boundaries even further. Whether you need to perform detailed retouching, compositing, or intricate masking, Photoshop offers tools that Lightroom cannot match. But the beauty of Adobe's ecosystem is that you don't have to choose between these two powerful programs—they work seamlessly together, allowing you to enhance your photos in ways that would be nearly impossible with Lightroom alone.

For many photographers, the workflow begins in Lightroom Classic. You import, organize, and perform basic edits such as adjusting exposure, white balance, and sharpness. Once you've optimized your image in Lightroom and are ready to take it to the next level, you can easily pass it off to Photoshop for more advanced techniques. In this section, we'll walk you through how to integrate Lightroom with Photoshop, providing a smooth and efficient workflow for all your editing needs.

The Lightroom to Photoshop Workflow

The integration between Lightroom and Photoshop is incredibly straightforward. Once you've made your basic adjustments in Lightroom, you can send your image to Photoshop with a single click. Here's how it works:

1. **Select Your Image in Lightroom**: Start by selecting the image you want to work on in Lightroom's Library or Develop module.

2. **Open in Photoshop**: Right-click on the selected image and choose **Edit In > Edit in Photoshop**. Alternatively, you can use the keyboard shortcut **Cmd + E** (Mac) or **Ctrl + E** (Windows). Lightroom will automatically open the image in Photoshop, where you can perform advanced edits.

3. **Save the Edited Image**: After you've finished editing in Photoshop, save the file as you would with any Photoshop project. Once saved, the image will automatically be saved back into Lightroom as a new file, preserving your original image. Lightroom also provides the option to save the edited file as a **PSD**, **TIFF**, or **JPEG** depending on your needs.

By seamlessly passing an image from Lightroom to Photoshop, you ensure that you maintain the non-destructive editing workflow that Lightroom offers, while taking full advantage of the advanced tools and features available in Photoshop. This integration allows you to enhance your creativity and push the boundaries of your editing skills.

Common Photoshop Tasks in Lightroom Workflow

There are certain tasks that are better suited for Photoshop due to its advanced features. These include:

- **Detailed Retouching**: Use Photoshop's healing brush, clone stamp, and content-aware tools for retouching skin, removing unwanted objects, or fixing imperfections that are difficult to achieve in Lightroom.

- **Layered Compositing**: If you need to combine multiple images or create complex compositions, Photoshop's layer-based workflow is essential. For example, merging bracketed exposures for HDR or creating panoramas.

- **Advanced Masking and Selections**: Photoshop allows you to perform intricate selections and apply complex masks, which can be especially useful for portrait retouching or when working with complex subjects.

By sending your image from Lightroom to Photoshop, you have access to these tools, giving you the best of both worlds: Lightroom's powerful organizational features and Photoshop's unparalleled editing capabilities.

EXPORTING AND PREPARING IMAGES FOR PRINT OR WEB

Once your editing process is complete, the next critical step is **exporting** your images. Whether you plan to showcase your work on social media, create a portfolio, or prepare images for a client, exporting is a crucial step that ensures your images are ready for delivery in the best possible format. Lightroom Classic offers extensive options for exporting images in a variety of formats, sizes, and resolutions.

In this section, we'll dive deep into the art of **exporting images**, covering everything from preparing images for the web and social media to preparing high-quality prints. Understanding how to properly export your images will help ensure they look their best wherever they are displayed.

Preparing Images for the Web

The web is one of the most common places to showcase your work, whether it's for your personal portfolio, a social media profile, or a commercial website. Lightroom Classic gives you several options to export images in a web-friendly format that optimizes both **file size** and **quality**. Here's how to export images for web use:

1. **Image Size and Resolution**: For web use, it's important to ensure your images are optimized for fast loading times without sacrificing quality. In the **Export** dialog box, select **JPEG** as the file format. For web images, a resolution of **72 PPI** (pixels per inch) is generally sufficient. You can also adjust the image dimensions (height and width) to fit the layout of your website or social media platform.

2. **Compression Settings**: Lightroom offers an option to adjust the **quality** of the JPEG file. Lowering the quality will reduce the file size, but too much compression can lead to noticeable pixelation or degradation in detail. It's important to strike a balance between size and quality. For most web images, setting the quality slider to **80-85%** works well for a good balance between compression and visual quality.

3. **Sharpening**: When exporting for web use, applying light **output sharpening** is recommended to counteract the slight loss of sharpness that can occur during export. Lightroom allows you to choose between **standard**, **low**, and **high** output sharpening based on your image's size and intended use.

4. **Metadata and Watermarks**: When exporting for the web, you may choose to **embed metadata** (such as copyright information) in the image file. Additionally, you can apply a **watermark** to protect your work from unauthorized use.

Preparing Images for Print

Exporting images for print is a different process entirely. Prints require higher resolution images, typically **300 PPI**, and larger file sizes. Whether you're printing a small photo for a client or creating a large-format art piece, Lightroom's export options allow you to deliver images at the best possible quality.

1. **Resolution and Dimensions**: For prints, you'll want to export at a resolution of **300 PPI** to ensure high-quality prints. Adjust the image dimensions to match the print size you want (e.g., 8x10 inches, 16x20 inches, etc.). If you're unsure about the print size, it's better to export at a higher resolution to avoid any quality loss.

2. **Color Space**: For print, you should use **Adobe RGB** or **ProPhoto RGB** as your color space. These color spaces offer a wider gamut than sRGB (which is used for the web) and ensure better color reproduction in print.

3. **Sharpening for Print**: Lightroom provides the option to apply **sharpening for print**, which is useful to bring out fine details that may be lost during the printing process. Lightroom allows you to select different types of sharpening based on the type of paper you plan to print on (e.g., glossy, matte).

4. **File Format**: TIFF is often recommended for print due to its high-quality, lossless nature. However, you can also use **JPEG** for print, especially if you need smaller file sizes. If you use JPEG, make sure to select **maximum quality** to avoid compression artifacts.

SYNCING LIGHTROOM WITH ADOBE CREATIVE CLOUD

In today's digital workflow, having your photos accessible across multiple devices is more important than ever. Lightroom Classic 2025 provides seamless integration with **Adobe Creative Cloud**, which allows you to sync your photos between Lightroom Classic and Lightroom CC on your desktop, mobile devices, or web. This functionality can greatly improve your workflow, giving you the freedom to edit and manage your images on the go.

Setting Up Syncing

To begin syncing, you first need to ensure you have an active **Adobe Creative Cloud** subscription. Once subscribed, you can enable syncing within the Lightroom Classic interface. In the **Library** module, you'll see an option to enable **Sync with Lightroom**. After enabling sync, Lightroom Classic will start uploading your photos to Adobe's cloud, making them accessible from any device that supports Lightroom, including **smartphones**, **tablets**, and **the web**.

Benefits of Syncing

Syncing with Creative Cloud allows you to access your entire photo library from anywhere. Whether you're traveling and want to edit a photo on your tablet, or need to access a specific image from your phone while meeting with a client, syncing ensures that all your photos are just a click away. This can be especially helpful for photographers who need to deliver photos quickly or make edits while on the move.

Additionally, syncing between Lightroom Classic and Lightroom CC allows you to edit on one device and then continue working on another without missing a beat. Edits made on your desktop in Lightroom Classic sync to the cloud, where they can be accessed on your mobile devices. Similarly, changes made in Lightroom CC sync back to Lightroom Classic.

Syncing Smart Previews

When syncing photos from Lightroom Classic to Creative Cloud, Lightroom uploads **Smart Previews** rather than the full-size images. These smaller, compressed versions of your photos allow for fast editing on mobile devices without taking up too much cloud storage space. When you're back at your desktop, Lightroom Classic automatically updates the full-sized image, ensuring you have access to the highest quality file when needed.

SMART PREVIEWS: WORKING WITHOUT ORIGINAL FILES

Sometimes, you may find yourself in a situation where you need to work on your images but don't have access to the original files. Whether you're editing on a laptop during travel or working on an older project, **Smart Previews** in Lightroom Classic 2025 provide a solution. Smart Previews are smaller versions of your original files that retain much of the image's detail and quality, allowing you to edit without requiring access to the original files.

What Are Smart Previews?

Smart Previews are JPEG or DNG files that Lightroom creates for each image in your catalog. These smaller files are typically around 2-3 MB in size, compared to the full-size images, making them ideal for working in locations where bandwidth or storage space is limited. Smart Previews allow you to edit your photos as if you were working with the original file.

Creating and Using Smart Previews

To create a Smart Preview, you can simply select the images in Lightroom and choose **Library > Previews > Build Smart Previews**. Once the previews are built, you can start editing them just as you would with the full-sized images. Lightroom will keep track of any changes you make, and when the original files become available, it will sync the edits automatically.

The ability to work with Smart Previews is an invaluable feature for photographers on the go, offering the flexibility to edit from anywhere. Whether you're in a remote location with limited access to your original files or you need to travel light, Smart Previews ensure you can continue your workflow without interruption.

LIGHTROOM MOBILE INTEGRATION AND EDITING ON THE GO

In today's world of mobile technology, photographers are no longer tied to their desktops for photo editing. Adobe Lightroom Classic 2025 offers **seamless integration with Lightroom Mobile**, which allows you to edit and manage your photos on the go using your smartphone or tablet. Whether you're traveling or need to deliver images quickly to a client, Lightroom Mobile puts the power of Lightroom in the palm of your hand.

Getting Started with Lightroom Mobile

To use Lightroom Mobile, simply download the app on your **iOS** or **Android** device. Once installed, sign in using your Adobe ID, and Lightroom will automatically sync your photos and edits across devices through **Adobe Creative Cloud**. You can upload your images from Lightroom Classic to Lightroom Mobile, and any edits made on the mobile app will sync back to your desktop version.

Editing on the Go

With Lightroom Mobile, you can access all the basic and advanced editing tools you're used to in the desktop version, including **exposure adjustments**, **cropping**, **color grading**, and **masking**. While the mobile interface may feel slightly different from the desktop, it's surprisingly powerful, giving you the flexibility to edit while on location.

Advantages of Lightroom Mobile

The biggest advantage of Lightroom Mobile is its ability to sync with Lightroom Classic. This means you can start editing a photo on your phone while traveling, and then finish the work on your desktop once you're back. It also offers the convenience of **sharing images** directly from the app to social media platforms, clients, or colleagues, making it a great tool for quickly delivering photos.

For photographers who shoot and edit in the field, Lightroom Mobile is a game-changer. It allows you to stay connected to your work even when you're away from your primary workstation, ensuring you never miss an opportunity to perfect your photos.

In this chapter, we've explored how to integrate **Lightroom Classic 2025** with other **Adobe tools** to create a smooth, efficient workflow. From using **Photoshop** for advanced editing to syncing images across devices via **Creative Cloud**, Lightroom Classic's integration with other Adobe software and services enables photographers to achieve more, work faster, and stay productive in any environment.

The addition of **Smart Previews** and **Lightroom Mobile** ensures that you can continue your work, whether you're at your desk or on the go. By mastering these integration features, you can enhance your editing process and make your photography workflow more flexible, organized, and efficient.

CHAPTER 9: TROUBLESHOOTING AND COMMON LIGHTROOM ISSUES

SOLVING PERFORMANCE ISSUES AND SPEED OPTIMIZATION

As with any powerful software, **Adobe Lightroom Classic 2025** can sometimes experience performance slowdowns, especially when handling large image libraries, heavy processing tasks, or intricate edits. Understanding how to optimize Lightroom for speed is crucial for any photographer who values efficiency and smooth workflow. Whether you're working with a handful of images or thousands, having a system that runs quickly and efficiently can save hours of work and frustration.

Understanding Lightroom's System Requirements

Before diving into troubleshooting, it's important to ensure that your system meets the **minimum and recommended system requirements** for Lightroom Classic 2025. While Lightroom can run on most modern computers, performance will depend heavily on your hardware, particularly your **processor (CPU)**, **memory (RAM)**, and **graphics card (GPU)**.

Lightroom requires substantial processing power when handling high-resolution images or complex edits, and having an underpowered computer can result in slowdowns. If you're working with raw files, especially those from high-megapixel cameras, upgrading your hardware could be the first step toward improved performance.

Here's a breakdown of the key components that impact Lightroom's speed:

- **Processor (CPU)**: Lightroom is a multi-threaded program, meaning it benefits from multiple processor cores. The faster the processor, the quicker Lightroom will render previews, apply adjustments, and handle large files.

- **Memory (RAM)**: Lightroom uses RAM to store image previews and process data. The more RAM you have, the smoother your experience will be, especially when working with large catalogs. **16 GB of RAM** is the minimum recommended, but **32 GB or more** is ideal for large libraries and intensive edits.

- **Graphics Card (GPU)**: Lightroom Classic 2025 offers **GPU acceleration** for tasks such as image rendering, the **develop module**, and **interactive adjustments**. A more powerful graphics card can greatly enhance performance, particularly when using **GPU-accelerated editing tools**.

Optimizing Lightroom's Performance Settings

After ensuring that your hardware meets the recommended specs, it's time to adjust **Lightroom's preferences** to get the best performance out of your system. Lightroom's **Performance Preferences** are located in the **Edit > Preferences > Performance** tab, where you can make adjustments to enhance its speed and responsiveness.

One of the most significant changes you can make is enabling **GPU acceleration**. By checking the **Use Graphics Processor** option, Lightroom can offload some of its graphical rendering to your GPU, reducing the workload on your CPU. This is especially beneficial when working with large images or performing tasks like zooming, panning, and applying adjustments.

Additionally, you should consider increasing the **Camera Raw Cache** size. This cache is where Lightroom stores previews of your images, allowing it to load them more quickly. Increasing the cache size (typically between **5 GB to 20 GB**) helps Lightroom access and process images faster.

Managing Catalog and Preview Settings

Another area where you can optimize performance is by managing your **catalog settings**. Lightroom stores all edits, metadata, and previews in the catalog file. Ensuring your catalog is properly optimized is critical to keeping Lightroom running smoothly.

To do this, go to **Catalog Settings** under **Edit > Catalog Settings**. There, you can choose how often Lightroom automatically backs up your catalog, which can impact performance. If you're experiencing slowdowns, try adjusting backup frequency to avoid excessive catalog writing.

Preview Management is another aspect of performance optimization. Lightroom generates **standard previews** and **1:1 previews** for each image, allowing faster zooming and navigation. However, these previews can take up significant disk space. You can adjust the quality and size of the previews in the **File Handling** section of the Preferences panel to reduce the amount of space Lightroom uses.

Reducing Lag and Improving Workflow

If you're experiencing **lag** while editing or moving through your library, here are a few additional steps to boost speed:

- **Use Smart Previews**: Smart Previews are smaller versions of your images, allowing you to edit photos without needing access to the original files. They speed up editing and allow Lightroom to work efficiently even when your originals are stored on external drives or are offline.

- **Declutter Your Catalog**: Large catalogs with too many images can slow Lightroom down. Consider **splitting catalogs** for specific projects or clients to reduce the load. Additionally, periodically **optimizing your catalog** (by going to **File > Optimize Catalog**) can help maintain performance.

By implementing these optimization strategies, you can significantly improve Lightroom's performance, making your editing experience more seamless and enjoyable.

RESOLVING IMPORT AND EXPORT PROBLEMS

As essential as the import and export processes are in Lightroom, they can occasionally cause headaches. Whether it's a failed import, missing files, or errors during the export process, issues can arise that disrupt the flow of your work. Understanding the root causes of these problems and knowing how to resolve them is crucial for maintaining a smooth workflow.

Troubleshooting Import Issues

Importing images into Lightroom Classic is a straightforward process, but several issues can prevent it from going smoothly. Common problems include:

- **Missing Files**: If Lightroom can't find your images after importing, it might be because the files have been moved or renamed outside of Lightroom.

Lightroom keeps track of files based on their location, so if the file's path changes, it can no longer locate the photo. To fix this, go to the **Library module**, and Lightroom will prompt you to **locate the missing file** by browsing your computer.

- **Corrupted or Unsupported Files**: Occasionally, a corrupt image file may prevent Lightroom from importing it. If Lightroom cannot open the image, it may be due to a file corruption issue. You can try opening the file in another program (like Photoshop) to confirm whether the file is damaged. If the file is corrupt, you may need to recover it or re-shoot it.

- **Import Preferences**: If Lightroom fails to import images from a camera or external drive, check your import preferences under **Edit > Preferences > General**. Ensure that your source devices are correctly recognized and that **automated import actions**, such as applying metadata or renaming files, are configured correctly.

Export Problems and Solutions

Exporting images is often the final step in your workflow, but export errors can occur. Here are some common issues and fixes:

- **Export Failures**: If Lightroom fails to export an image, it could be due to issues with your **destination folder**, incorrect file format selection, or export settings that conflict with the file. Ensure that the export destination has write permissions and enough available storage space.

- **Exporting with Incorrect Settings**: Sometimes, the exported images may not match your intended settings. This is usually due to incorrect settings in the **Export dialog box**. Double-check options like **file format (JPEG, TIFF, PNG), color space (sRGB, AdobeRGB)**, and **output sharpening**. Ensuring the correct resolution for print or web is also vital to avoid exporting at the wrong quality.

- **Image Quality Loss During Export**: One common issue when exporting is a noticeable loss of image quality, especially when resizing or compressing for the web. To avoid this, ensure that the **Export Quality** slider is set to

100% for maximum output quality. Avoid heavy compression and keep an eye on the **resolution** (72 PPI for web, 300 PPI for print).

By thoroughly checking your import and export settings, and resolving any file issues, you can ensure that Lightroom performs these essential tasks without a hitch.

HOW TO FIX CORRUPTED CATALOGS

A **corrupted catalog** can be a photographer's worst nightmare. Your Lightroom catalog holds all your edits, metadata, and organization for your images, so when it becomes corrupted, it can result in data loss and a disrupted workflow. Luckily, there are ways to fix or recover a corrupted catalog, and understanding how to prevent it in the future can save you a lot of stress.

Signs of a Corrupted Catalog

Before delving into solutions, it's important to recognize the signs of a corrupted catalog. These include:

- Lightroom crashing when you try to open the catalog.

- Missing or mismatched image previews.

- The inability to perform basic tasks, like importing, exporting, or applying adjustments.

- Error messages related to the catalog when attempting to launch Lightroom.

Fixing a Corrupted Catalog

If you suspect that your catalog has become corrupted, the first step is to try to recover it using Lightroom's built-in recovery options.

1. **Use the Catalog Backup**: Lightroom automatically backs up your catalog at intervals you set (usually when you exit the program). If you've enabled **automatic backups**, you can restore the catalog from the most recent backup. To do this, go to **File > Open Catalog** and choose the backup file.

2. **Create a New Catalog**: If you can't recover your catalog, you can create a new one. However, the images in the original catalog might be intact. After creating a new catalog, you can attempt to import images from the damaged catalog, which should allow you to salvage your work.

3. **Optimize the Catalog**: If your catalog is not severely corrupted, you can try **optimizing it** to fix performance issues. Go to **File > Optimize Catalog**, which can help resolve minor corruption and speed up the catalog's performance.

4. **Rebuild the Previews**: If the images in the catalog appear but with missing or broken previews, you can **rebuild the previews** by going to the **Library > Previews** section and selecting **Build 1:1 Previews**. This can help restore the visual aspect of your catalog.

Preventing Future Catalog Corruption

To prevent future catalog corruption, here are some best practices:

- **Regular Backups**: Always back up your catalog regularly to a separate hard drive or cloud storage. Make sure you store backups of both your catalog and images in different physical locations.

- **Limit Simultaneous Access**: Avoid opening the same catalog on multiple devices at the same time. This can lead to corruption due to conflicting changes.

- **Catalog Maintenance**: Periodically optimize your catalog, clean up unnecessary previews, and ensure that Lightroom is properly closed each time to avoid corruption.

By taking these precautions, you can greatly reduce the risk of catalog corruption and ensure that your valuable work remains safe.

COMMON EDITING MISTAKES AND HOW TO FIX THEM

Even experienced photographers make editing mistakes, whether it's applying too much contrast, adjusting white balance incorrectly, or losing focus on the original composition. Fortunately, Lightroom provides a non-destructive editing workflow, so most mistakes can be easily corrected. Let's explore some common editing mistakes and how to fix them.

Overdoing Contrast or Exposure Adjustments

One of the most common editing mistakes is **over-adjusting contrast or exposure**. This can lead to loss of detail in both the shadows and highlights, resulting in an unnatural look. If you've overdone your contrast or exposure, Lightroom gives you the ability to **reset** the sliders or fine-tune them back to a more balanced setting.

To fix this mistake, use the **History panel** to go back to a previous step where the adjustments were less extreme, or use the **Reset** button in the **Basic Panel** to return all settings to their default values.

Incorrect White Balance

An incorrectly adjusted **white balance** can make your image look too warm (yellow/orange) or too cool (blue). If you find that your whites look off, you can use the **White Balance** sliders in the **Basic Panel** to correct the color cast. Alternatively, use the **Eyedropper Tool** to select a neutral area in the image (like a white or gray object), which Lightroom will use to automatically correct the white balance.

Unnatural Skin Tones

When editing portraits, getting the **skin tone right** is crucial. Over-saturating skin tones or using overly aggressive editing tools can make the subject look unnatural. To fix skin tones, consider using the **HSL panel** to adjust the **Hue** and **Saturation** of the **Red** and **Orange** sliders, which directly affect skin tones. Subtle tweaks can bring out more natural-looking skin without making it look too overdone.

BACKUP AND RESTORE: PROTECTING YOUR CATALOG AND EDITS

Finally, no matter how efficient your workflow is, ensuring that your work is **properly backed up** is essential to protecting your valuable photos and edits. Losing your Lightroom catalog or images due to a hardware failure, accidental deletion, or corruption can be devastating. In this section, we'll cover how to effectively **backup** and **restore** your Lightroom catalog and images to keep your workflow safe and secure.

Backing Up Your Lightroom Catalog

Lightroom Classic has a built-in catalog backup system that automatically creates backups of your catalog at regular intervals. It's crucial to enable this feature and store your backups in a secure location, whether it's an external hard drive or cloud storage. You can customize your backup settings by going to **Edit > Catalog Settings > Backup**, where you can choose how often Lightroom backs up the catalog and where to store those backups.

Backing Up Your Images

In addition to backing up your catalog, make sure to **back up your image files** as well. Lightroom only tracks the location of your images—it doesn't actually store them. Therefore, it's essential to store your photos in multiple locations (e.g., external drives or cloud services) to safeguard them against data loss.

Restoring Your Catalog and Images

If you ever encounter a situation where your catalog is corrupted or lost, you can easily restore it from a backup. To restore a catalog, go to **File > Open Catalog**, and choose your backup file. If your images are lost or corrupted, having a backup of your files means you won't have to start from scratch.

By regularly backing up your catalog and images, you can ensure that your work is always safe and accessible, even in the event of unexpected issues.

Troubleshooting and resolving common issues in Lightroom Classic 2025 is an essential part of any photographer's workflow. From performance optimization to solving import/export problems and fixing corrupted catalogs, understanding how to handle these challenges will save you time and stress. By being proactive with backups, knowing how to resolve editing mistakes, and optimizing Lightroom for speed, you can ensure a smoother, more efficient experience.

With the right troubleshooting strategies in place, you'll be able to keep your Lightroom workflow running smoothly and focus on what you do best—editing and creating beautiful images.

CHAPTER 10: PRO TIPS FOR CREATING STUNNING FINAL IMAGES

COLOR GRADING FOR CINEMATIC LOOKS

When it comes to creating stunning final images, one of the most powerful techniques in your Lightroom toolkit is **color grading**. The use of color to evoke mood and style is an art form in itself, especially when striving for a cinematic look. Think of the golden hour glow in a film scene or the stark contrast of deep shadows and warm highlights in a thriller—these are not just random color choices, but meticulously designed color schemes that enhance the narrative and emotional impact of an image. In Lightroom Classic 2025, you have the tools to achieve these kinds of looks, whether you're working with portraits, landscapes, or conceptual imagery.

Color grading allows you to influence the overall feel of an image by adjusting its color palette. This can range from subtle tweaks that enhance natural colors to bold shifts that create a more dramatic or stylized result. Whether you're going for a **vintage** look, a **moody cinematic vibe**, or a **vibrant pop of color**, understanding how to apply color grading effectively is essential for photographers who want to take their edits to the next level.

In Lightroom, **color grading** is made accessible through tools like the **HSL panel**, **Tone Curve**, and **Color Grading Panel**. These tools allow you to tweak individual colors, adjust shadows, highlights, and midtones, and apply global color shifts for a more cohesive look. As you work through this chapter, you'll learn how to manipulate these settings to create a cinematic atmosphere that draws the viewer in and gives your photos a professional, polished finish.

The ability to use **color to tell a story** is one of the most important skills a photographer can develop, and with Lightroom Classic 2025's powerful color grading features, you have everything you need to create images that stand out. From warm vintage tones to cool, moody contrasts, color grading can help you craft the exact look you're aiming for—whether you're editing for personal expression or client work.

Understanding Color Grading Tools in Lightroom

Let's take a deeper look at the key tools available in Lightroom Classic 2025 for creating cinematic looks. These tools will enable you to manipulate your image's color palette with precision and creativity.

HSL Panel: The **HSL** (Hue, Saturation, and Luminance) panel is the primary tool for adjusting colors individually. This panel allows you to control how each color appears in your image. For example, you can make the greens in your landscape pop with increased saturation, or cool down the warm skin tones in a portrait by tweaking the red hues.

Hue: Shifts the color itself. If you want a more orange sunset, you can shift the yellow hues toward red.

Saturation: Controls the intensity of a color. You can desaturate distracting colors or enhance certain hues for dramatic effect.

Luminance: Affects the brightness of colors. For example, darkening the blues in a sky can add contrast, while brightening them can make the scene feel airy and light.

Tone Curve: The **Tone Curve** tool is excellent for creating deep contrasts or fine-tuning shadows, midtones, and highlights. A cinematic look often involves deep shadows and slightly elevated highlights to create a balanced, dynamic range that evokes drama. Adjusting the tone curve to add an **S-curve** (by pulling down the shadows and lifting the highlights) can increase contrast and give your image a more film-like feel. You can also apply curves to specific channels (Red, Green, Blue) to add subtle color casts to different parts of the tonal range.

Color Grading Panel: The **Color Grading Panel** offers more advanced color manipulation, allowing you to tweak the **shadows**, **midtones**, and **highlights** separately. This panel is ideal for creating the type of **split-toning** effect seen in cinematic photography, where the shadows may have one color cast (like blue or teal), and the highlights are warmed up with orange or yellow hues. By applying color to each tonal range, you can achieve a balanced yet dramatic cinematic look.

Shadows: Adding a cooler tone to the shadows (e.g., teal) and a warm tone to the highlights (e.g., orange) is one of the classic cinematic looks.

Midtones: Often, you want to keep the midtones more neutral to retain the subject's natural colors while adjusting the extremes (shadows and highlights).

Highlights: Bright highlights can be enhanced with warm tones to evoke a feeling of warmth and light.

Vibrance and Saturation: For cinematic effects, **vibrance** can be used to selectively boost more muted colors, while **saturation** applies a global increase to all colors. Vibrance is particularly useful when you want to enhance specific hues without making the image feel overly saturated, preserving skin tones in portraits, for example.

By combining these tools effectively, you can create cinematic color grades that give your images a dramatic and professional look. Whether you're enhancing a sunset or giving a portrait a moody, film-inspired edit, color grading is one of the most impactful ways to elevate your editing skills.

CREATIVE EFFECTS: VIGNETTES, SPLIT TONING, AND MORE

In addition to color grading, **creative effects** like **vignettes**, **split toning**, and other techniques play a significant role in giving your images a polished, professional finish. These tools allow you to manipulate the image in creative ways, enhancing the mood and making your subject stand out. Whether you want to focus the viewer's attention on the center of the image, create a vintage look, or add an artistic flair, Lightroom Classic provides several creative tools to help you achieve these effects.

Creating Vignettes

A **vignette** is a gradual darkening or lightening of the image's corners and edges, which directs the viewer's eye toward the center of the photo. Vignettes can add a subtle or dramatic effect, depending on how much you apply. Lightroom Classic offers both **post-crop vignetting** and **radial vignetting**, each with its own purpose.

Post-Crop Vignetting: This is the most common vignette tool, and it works by darkening the edges of the image after cropping. You can adjust the **amount** (how dark or light the vignette is), the **midpoint** (how far the vignette extends into the image), and the **roundness** (how circular or oval the vignette is). This is great for emphasizing your subject or adding a moody, dramatic effect.

Radial Vignetting: For more control, the **Radial Filter** lets you create a circular vignette around a specific part of your image. You can adjust the size, shape, and feathering of the vignette, as well as invert the effect if you want to brighten the center rather than darken it.

When used properly, vignettes can create a sense of depth and focus, drawing attention to the main subject of your image.

Split Toning for Creative Color Effects

Split toning is a classic technique in both film and digital photography where different colors are applied to the **shadows** and **highlights** of an image. The result is a subtle yet striking color shift that can add mood and character to your photos. In Lightroom Classic 2025, split toning is made easy through the **Color Grading Panel**, where you can independently adjust the **shadows**, **midtones**, and **highlights** using the **hue** and **saturation** sliders.

For example, in landscape photography, you might want to add a cool tone to the shadows (such as teal or blue) to evoke a serene, early morning atmosphere, while warming up the highlights with a golden hue to simulate the glow of a sunrise. In portraiture, you could use a more neutral look with slight splits in the shadows and highlights to create a natural and flattering effect.

By applying split toning, you can give your images a vintage look, enhance the mood, or simply create a more visually dynamic photo that stands out from the crowd.

Other Creative Effects: Grain and Texture

Another creative effect to consider is the addition of **grain**, which simulates the look of film. Lightroom allows you to control the **size** and **roughness** of the grain, enabling you to add a subtle texture to your images for a more organic, vintage feel. This is particularly effective when working with black-and-white conversions or when trying to replicate the look of classic film photography.

You can also use the **Texture** and **Clarity** sliders to enhance fine details in your image. While **Clarity** increases contrast in the midtones, **Texture** focuses on enhancing the fine details of surfaces like skin, fabric, or landscapes. These adjustments can bring out intricate details, adding depth to your image.

ENHANCING DETAILS WITH THE CLARITY AND TEXTURE SLIDERS

When it comes to refining your images and bringing out subtle details, the **Clarity** and **Texture** sliders in Lightroom Classic 2025 are indispensable tools. These sliders can give your images more depth and dimension, improving the overall sharpness without compromising the image's natural appearance. While both tools work on similar principles, they differ in their application and results.

The Clarity Slider

The **Clarity** slider is designed to enhance midtone contrast, making textures and details in the midtones more prominent. Increasing clarity adds a sense of crispness and sharpness, making surfaces like skin, hair, or textured surfaces (like brick walls or foliage) stand out. However, too much clarity can result in an overly harsh or "HDR-like" appearance, which can be undesirable in certain contexts.

In portrait photography, **increasing clarity** can help define facial features and texture, but it should be used subtly. In landscapes, increasing clarity can enhance the texture of clouds, mountains, and foliage. However, it's important to use clarity sparingly to avoid introducing unwanted artifacts, particularly in smooth areas like skin.

The Texture Slider

The **Texture** slider is a more refined version of clarity, focusing on fine details in the image. Unlike clarity, which affects midtone contrast globally, **Texture** enhances or softens the fine details in the image. This makes it particularly useful for subtle adjustments that affect specific parts of an image without altering the overall contrast.

For example, if you're editing a portrait, the **Texture** slider can enhance skin details without making the subject look overly sharpened. If you're editing landscapes, increasing the texture can bring out the intricate details in foliage or water without making the image look overly harsh.

Both the clarity and texture sliders are essential tools for bringing out fine details and enhancing the depth of your image, making them an integral part of your editing toolkit.

FINALIZING YOUR WORKFLOW FOR CONSISTENCY

Consistency is key to creating a professional-looking portfolio or maintaining a cohesive style across a series of images. In this section, we'll explore how to **finalize your workflow** to ensure that each image in your catalog maintains a uniform look, making it easier to present a cohesive set of images to clients or showcase your work.

Applying Presets Across Multiple Images

One of the best ways to maintain consistency across multiple images is by using **presets**. Lightroom Classic 2025 allows you to create and apply custom presets that contain a combination of settings, such as exposure adjustments, color grading, and other edits. Applying the same preset to multiple images ensures that they all share the same basic adjustments, saving you time and ensuring a cohesive style.

For example, if you're editing a wedding shoot, you can create a preset that gives your images a soft, vintage look with warm tones and soft contrast. By applying this preset to all the photos in the shoot, you create a uniform style that will make the collection of images feel cohesive and polished.

Syncing Settings for Consistency

In addition to using presets, you can **synchronize settings** across multiple images. This is especially useful when you have a set of images that require the same adjustments, such as a group of portraits or a series of product shots. Lightroom allows you to sync settings like exposure, white balance, and even local adjustments between multiple photos. Simply select the image you've edited, click the **Sync** button, and apply the same settings to the other selected images.

Creating a Consistent Look with Collections

Using **collections** is another great way to organize your images by style or theme, ensuring that your final output is consistent. Lightroom's **smart collections** can automatically group images based on specific criteria, such as star ratings, keywords, or even metadata. This helps keep your workflow organized, making it easier to apply a consistent style across your entire catalog.

EXPORTING FOR PROFESSIONAL RESULTS

Once your image is edited and finalized, the next step is **exporting** it. How you export your images will depend on your intended output, whether it's for web, print, or sharing on social media. Lightroom offers a wide range of export options that allow you to deliver professional-quality results tailored to your specific needs.

Preparing for Print

When exporting for print, you'll need to consider the resolution, color space, and file format. For print, you'll want to use a **300 PPI (pixels per inch)** resolution to ensure high-quality output. The **AdobeRGB** color space is also ideal for print, as it offers a wider gamut of colors than sRGB. Export your images as **TIFF** or **JPEG** files, depending on the print medium.

Exporting for Web and Social Media

For web and social media, the goal is to strike a balance between quality and file size. **JPEG** is the standard format for online use, as it provides good quality with relatively small file sizes. For social media platforms like Instagram or Facebook, you'll want to ensure your images are exported at a resolution of **72 PPI** and resized to the optimal dimensions for each platform. Lightroom allows you to apply **output sharpening** for web images to enhance details after resizing.

Customizing Export Settings with Presets

To speed up the export process, Lightroom lets you create custom **export presets**. If you frequently export images with the same settings, such as for a portfolio, a client, or a specific social media platform, you can save those settings as a preset. This allows you to apply them with a single click, ensuring consistency and saving time.

Creating stunning final images involves much more than just making basic adjustments; it's about refining your images, adding creative effects, and ensuring a professional finish. In this chapter, we've covered the essential techniques for achieving cinematic color grading, adding creative effects, enhancing details, maintaining consistency across your work, and exporting images for the best possible results.

By mastering these techniques, you'll be able to elevate your photography to a professional level, creating images that stand out and resonate with viewers. Whether you're preparing a portfolio, delivering client work, or sharing your creations with the world, the pro tips in this chapter will help you fine-tune your workflow and achieve the stunning results you've always envisioned.

APPENDICES

GLOSSARY OF LIGHTROOM CLASSIC TERMS

Understanding the terminology used in Lightroom Classic is essential for mastering its features and maximizing its potential. This glossary provides clear definitions of the most commonly used terms and concepts, helping you navigate Lightroom more effectively. Whether you're new to Lightroom or looking to brush up on your skills, this section will serve as a helpful reference throughout your workflow.

Catalog

A **catalog** is a database that stores references to your photos and the edits you've made to them. The catalog does not contain the images themselves; it simply holds information about their location, metadata, keywords, and edit history. It's important to regularly back up your catalog to avoid data loss.

Develop Module

The **Develop Module** is where you do the majority of your photo editing in Lightroom. This module provides tools for adjusting exposure, contrast, color, sharpness, and applying various effects to your photos. It's essential for any non-destructive editing you do in Lightroom.

Import

Import refers to the process of bringing new photos into Lightroom from your camera, memory card, hard drive, or other devices. During import, you can apply presets, keywords, and organize the images into folders or collections for easier access.

Metadata

Metadata refers to the information embedded in an image file that describes its content. This can include details such as the camera settings used (shutter speed, ISO, etc.), the location, date, and any other added tags or keywords. Lightroom allows you to view and modify the metadata for each image.

Smart Previews

Smart Previews are smaller versions of your original images that you can use to edit photos without needing access to the full-size files. They are especially useful when working on laptops or devices with limited storage, allowing you to continue editing even when the original images are stored elsewhere.

Adjustment Brush

The **Adjustment Brush** is a tool used in the **Develop Module** to apply local adjustments to specific areas of an image. This tool allows you to "paint" adjustments like exposure, contrast, or clarity onto selected areas of a photo for detailed editing.

Presets

Presets are pre-configured settings in Lightroom that apply a set of adjustments to an image with a single click. Lightroom comes with several default presets, and you can also create your own or download others. Presets are useful for speeding up your workflow and achieving a consistent style.

Collections

Collections are virtual groups of images within Lightroom that allow you to organize your photos. Unlike folders, collections don't affect the physical location of the images—they simply provide a way to group images based on specific criteria (e.g., a portfolio, a specific shoot, or images needing further editing).

Histogram

The **Histogram** is a graphical representation of the tonal range of an image. It shows the distribution of shadows, midtones, and highlights, helping you assess the exposure and contrast of your photo. The histogram is located in the **Develop Module** and is a crucial tool for evaluating your image adjustments.

Lens Corrections

Lens Corrections refers to the adjustments made to fix distortion, chromatic aberration, and vignetting caused by your lens. Lightroom has built-in profiles for many camera lenses, which automatically correct these issues. However, manual adjustments can also be made in the **Lens Corrections** panel.

Virtual Copy

A **Virtual Copy** is a duplicate of a photo in your catalog with different editing settings, but it does not take up additional space on your hard drive. Virtual copies allow you to experiment with different editing styles while preserving the original photo.

KEYBOARD SHORTCUTS FOR FASTER EDITING

Mastering Lightroom Classic's keyboard shortcuts can dramatically increase your editing speed and efficiency. The following are some of the most useful keyboard shortcuts for common tasks in Lightroom Classic. Incorporating these shortcuts into your workflow will help you edit more fluidly and with less reliance on the mouse.

Library Module Shortcuts

- **G**: Grid view

- **E**: Loupe view

- **F**: Full-screen view

- **Ctrl/Cmd + A**: Select all photos

- **Ctrl/Cmd + Shift + I**: Import photos

- **Ctrl/Cmd + Shift + E**: Export photos

Develop Module Shortcuts

- **D**: Switch to the Develop module

- **R**: Crop tool

- **Q**: Spot removal tool

- **Ctrl/Cmd + Z**: Undo last change

- **Ctrl/Cmd + Shift + Z**: Redo last change

- **Alt/Option + Shift + Ctrl/Cmd + E**: Merge to HDR

General Editing Shortcuts

- **+**: Increase exposure

- **-**: Decrease exposure

- **Ctrl/Cmd + Alt + Shift + N**: New catalog

- **Ctrl/Cmd + E**: Export

- **Ctrl/Cmd + Shift + P**: Toggle the clipping warnings (highlights and shadows)

- **Ctrl/Cmd + [**: Decrease brush size

- **Ctrl/Cmd +]**: Increase brush size

Navigational Shortcuts

- **Spacebar**: Toggle zoom tool

- **Ctrl/Cmd + Shift + F**: Show/Hide the Filmstrip

- **Ctrl/Cmd + /**: Toggle the panel on/off

Adjustment Shortcuts

- **Ctrl/Cmd + Alt + B**: Auto tone

- **Ctrl/Cmd + Shift + M**: Masking tools (new in Lightroom Classic 2025)

- **Shift + Tab**: Hide all panels (useful for maximizing editing space)

Incorporating these keyboard shortcuts into your editing routine will speed up repetitive tasks, making the editing process smoother and more efficient.

RECOMMENDED RESOURCES AND FURTHER READING

For photographers who want to dive deeper into Lightroom Classic 2025 and photo editing techniques, here are some recommended resources that will enhance your understanding and skills:

Books

1. **"The Adobe Photoshop Lightroom Classic CC Book for Digital Photographers" by Scott Kelby**

   This book is a comprehensive guide to Lightroom Classic, offering clear explanations and practical tips for photographers of all skill levels. Scott Kelby's engaging writing style makes this book easy to follow, even for beginners.

2. **"Lightroom Classic CC For Dummies" by Rob Sylvan**

   As part of the "For Dummies" series, this book breaks down Lightroom's features in an easy-to-understand format. It covers everything from basic adjustments to advanced techniques, making it a great resource for those new to Lightroom.

3. **"The Digital Photography Book" by Scott Kelby**

   Although this book focuses on digital photography in general, it includes invaluable tips for shooting and editing photos with Lightroom. The book also features useful insights from one of the most recognized names in photography.

4. **"Adobe Lightroom Classic: The Ultimate Guide to Digital Photography Post-Processing" by Michael Freeman**

   Freeman's book is a great resource for both beginners and intermediate Lightroom users. It offers a step-by-step approach to learning Lightroom, with practical examples and real-world editing scenarios.

Online Resources

1. **Adobe Lightroom Official Website**

   The Adobe website provides extensive resources on Lightroom Classic, including **tutorials**, **FAQ sections**, and **user guides**. It's an excellent place for exploring new features and learning best practices.

2. **KelbyOne**

   KelbyOne is an online learning platform that offers in-depth courses and tutorials on Lightroom Classic, taught by professional photographers and educators. It's perfect for photographers looking to advance their skills in both Lightroom and Photoshop.

3. **YouTube Tutorials**

   YouTube is a treasure trove of Lightroom tutorials. Channels like **Peter McKinnon**, **Phlearn**, and **Serge Ramelli Photography** offer easy-to-follow tutorials, tips, and tricks to help you master Lightroom and create stunning images.

4. **Lightroom Forums**

   Online forums, such as the **Adobe Lightroom Community** and **DPReview's Lightroom forum**, are great places to connect with other photographers, ask questions, and get advice on troubleshooting issues.

Websites for Presets and Plugins

1. **Presetpro.com**

   A site dedicated to premium Lightroom presets for various photography styles, including portrait, landscape, and wedding photography.

2. **Mastin Labs**

   Known for creating some of the best Lightroom presets that replicate classic film looks, Mastin Labs is a great resource for photographers who want to add a film-like quality to their digital images.

3. **Nik Collection by DxO**

   This collection of Lightroom and Photoshop plugins offers powerful editing tools like advanced color grading, noise reduction, and sharpening. It's an excellent addition for photographers looking to enhance their workflow.

TROUBLESHOOTING GUIDE FOR LIGHTROOM CLASSIC 2025

No software is perfect, and Lightroom Classic is no exception. From performance hiccups to missing files and other technical glitches, photographers occasionally run into problems while working with Lightroom. This troubleshooting guide offers practical solutions to the most common issues users face when using Lightroom Classic 2025.

1. Lightroom is Running Slowly or Freezing

Solution:

- **Optimize Your Catalog**: Go to **File > Optimize Catalog** to improve Lightroom's performance. Regular optimization helps reduce catalog corruption and slowdowns.

- **Use GPU Acceleration**: Make sure that **GPU acceleration** is enabled in **Preferences > Performance**. This will speed up tasks like image rendering and the application of adjustments.

- **Increase Camera Raw Cache**: In **Preferences > File Handling**, increase the **Camera Raw Cache** size. This will allow Lightroom to store more image data for faster access.

- **Clear the Cache**: If Lightroom is running slowly, clearing the cache might help. Go to **Preferences > Performance** and click **Purge Cache** to remove old data.

2. Images are Missing or Not Showing in Lightroom

Solution:

- **Relocate Missing Files**: If Lightroom can't find your images, it's likely because they were moved outside of Lightroom. Use the **Locate** function to point Lightroom to the new file location.

- **Check for Catalog Corruption**: If images are missing from your catalog, it could be a sign of catalog corruption. Try restoring your catalog from a recent backup.

- **Check File Permissions**: Ensure the images you're trying to import or edit have proper file permissions, especially if they are on an external drive or cloud storage.

3. Importing Issues: Photos Won't Import or Are Not Recognized

Solution:

- **Check File Type**: Ensure that the files you're importing are in a compatible format (such as **JPEG**, **TIFF**, **RAW**). Lightroom may not recognize unsupported file types.

- **Update Lightroom**: If your Lightroom version is outdated, certain camera models or file formats might not be supported. Make sure you're running the latest version of Lightroom Classic 2025.

- **Use the Import Dialog Box**: Sometimes the import process fails because Lightroom is not set to automatically recognize new devices. Open the **Import** dialog box manually by going to **File > Import Photos and Video** and selecting your source device.

4. Lightroom Crashes Frequently

Solution:

- **Update Software**: Make sure both **Lightroom Classic** and your **graphic drivers** are up to date. Adobe frequently releases bug fixes that may resolve crashing issues.

- **Check for Conflicting Plugins**: Disable any third-party plugins in Lightroom to see if they are causing crashes. Re-enable them one by one to identify the culprit.

- **Increase Memory Allocation**: If Lightroom is crashing due to low memory, try increasing the RAM allocation in **Preferences > Performance**.

5. Exporting Issues: Incorrect File Format or Resolution

Solution:

- **Double-Check Export Settings**: Ensure that you're exporting in the correct **file format** (JPEG, TIFF, etc.), and that the **resolution** is set correctly (e.g., **72 PPI** for web, **300 PPI** for print).

- **Adjust Color Space**: Make sure you're using the appropriate **color space** (sRGB for web, AdobeRGB or ProPhotoRGB for print). The wrong color space can lead to color discrepancies.

- **Check Export Destination**: Verify that your export destination has enough available space and that the path is not blocked by permissions or file conflicts.

This collection of appendices is designed to be a valuable resource for Lightroom Classic 2025 users. From a comprehensive glossary of terms to keyboard shortcuts that speed up your workflow, these sections offer everything you need to tackle challenges and maximize your Lightroom experience. The troubleshooting guide will help you resolve common issues, while the recommended resources and further reading will support your continued learning and mastery of Lightroom Classic.

By utilizing these appendices, you'll gain a deeper understanding of Lightroom's functionality and become more efficient in your photo editing, allowing you to focus more on your creative vision and less on technical challenges.

Printed in Dunstable, United Kingdom

71445263R00058